Design Your Dream Life is a must r̶̶̶ teachings that will give you the tools _____ ̲ your dream life and become all that you ar ___ ̲o be!
—PATTY AUBREY, *NEW YORK TIMES* BEST-SELLING AUTHOR
AND COFOUNDER OF THE CANFIELD TRAINING GROUP

Do you want to get over yourself and your self-limiting beliefs? Do you want to find out what is holding you back from the life you deserve? Denise's book is a must read if you've answered yes to these questions. This book gives us the answers that we have been searching for to build a better life.
—PAM SOWDER, COFOUNDER AND CHIEF NETWORKING
OFFICER, IT WORKS GLOBAL

The moment I opened this book I knew Denise had accomplished something great: a truly simple guide to learning how to live out your dreams and aspirations! This basic how-to manual, written in a simple and logical way, opens the door to the world of knowing how to accomplish your God-given dreams and goals in life.
—DR. STAN GRAVELY

Design Your Dream Life is something that every person with a dream needs. Denise gives thoughtful, practical, soul-stirring advice that inspires you to get moving toward the life you've always wanted. If you're through waiting for your moment, then now is the time to dig in with Denise and start building your dream.
—MERIDITH SIMES, PERSONAL GROWTH EXPERT AND
FORMER EDITOR-IN-CHIEF, *SUCCESS FROM HOME* MAGAZINE

Design Your Dream Life will shift your perspective and give you the tools you need to design your dream life. I have experienced the exercises within this book myself, and my life has been forever changed!
—CARLA BURNS, PHD, AUTHOR OF *WHAT WALT KNEW*

Design Your Dream Life is something so many people need and are searching for but haven't been able to find. Denise brilliantly leads readers through the process of identifying and working through self-limiting thoughts and beliefs, then activating their God-given dreams. For those who make the commitment, this book will change the course of each reader's future, replacing it with a dream life they may never have realized was possible until now.

—KIM T., ORLANDO, FL

I have read several books about designing the life you want. However, I often finished feeling more confused. Denise has a way of casting a vision, adding real-life examples, and offering exercises for you to do right in the here and now. I now have a clear vision. I know that I can excel in *every* area of my life—not just survive but truly thrive. I know what I want and how I'm going to get it. I couldn't be more excited!

—AMANDA C., DES MOINES, IA

I don't think I'll ever be able to thank you enough. What you have taught me was completely life changing. I've finally been able to breathe, and it has been about fifteen years since I've felt like this. Thank you from the bottom of my heart. Because of you, I *am*.

—SARAH R., LANSING, MI

design your
Dream
Life

Katie
Dream
Big!

design
your
Dream
Life

An Inspired Action Plan for Getting Unstuck and
Becoming Your Best Self

DENISE WALSH

DESIGN YOUR DREAM LIFE by Denise Walsh
1006 Cherry St SE
Grand Rapids, MI 49506
hello@denisewalsh.com

Copyright © 2019 by Denise Walsh
All rights reserved

Visit the author's website at DeniseWalsh.com.

International Standard Book Number: 978-0-692-15615-5

19 20 21 22 23 — 9 8 7 6 5 4 3 2
Printed in the United States of America

Contents

Acknowledgments

I AM FOREVER GRATEFUL to those who supported my vision, kept me going when I wanted to give up, and spoke life into me throughout this journey.

Special thanks to:

- My husband, Brandon, and my two red-headed little boys, who are my rock and my *why*.

- My mom and dad, for always being the best mom and dad I could ask for.

- My It Works family and mentors, Kami Pentecost, Mark and Cindy Pentecost, Pam Sowder, and Mike Potillo. Thank you for casting vision and giving me a place to grow.

- My friends Lisa Thompson, Amanda Cozad, Shyanne Herbert, Renee Hays, Nicholas Kimps, and Carla Burns, who read through my early manuscripts, gave me feedback, sent me articles and videos to help with research, and rode the learning wave with me. I am forever grateful for your support, encouragement, and feedback.

- The Train the Trainer community with Jack Canfield and specifically my mastermind group, who held me accountable and consistently helped me to brainstorm throughout this project. Everyone needs a team of people to kick their butt sometimes.

Last, this project could not have been completed without the support of my writing coach, Lisa Jimenez; product development and marketing team, including Amanda Quain, Woodley Auguste, Ziev Beresh, and Donna Scuderi; and event planner, Carlos Kulas-Dominguez.

Oh, and I cannot forget—thank You, Holy Spirit, for not only whispering to me throughout the development and creation of this workbook but during the years prior. You guided me and opened my eyes to things I might not have understood otherwise, and for that I am eternally grateful.

Introduction

I'M SURE BY now you've heard it all: "Work smarter, not harder." "Take massive action." "Lean in to your strengths." "Don't give up." "Learn to love yourself." "Just make it happen." "Aim higher." "Manage your time better." This advice is fine. But it isn't what you really need. It isn't the sort of concrete wisdom that will get you unstuck from the same old, same old that you can't seem to break out of. It isn't what you need when you can't figure out why even though you've been working your tail off, the next level of success seems to stay just out of your grasp. It won't help you put your finger on what it is about your marriage or career path that just isn't quite right so that you can make the change that will shift everything for the better. It doesn't tell you what you have to know in order to pursue the life of your dreams and start living it.

The truth is, there is a specific path that leads to success, and—no disrespect to Confucius or those who love to quote him—statements like, "It does not matter how slowly you go as long as you do not stop," won't help you find it. That ambiguous kind of direction, which is oftentimes exactly the sort of thing you hear when you start asking specific questions about how to achieve success, belongs on motivational posters. But it doesn't contain the tools you need and can't teach you the strategies you must develop in order to live the successful, purposeful, fun life you were made to enjoy.

And make no mistake: You were made for a full, fulfilled life. The inner craving you feel for more? That's confirmation that where you are is not where you were meant to stay. Regardless of your age or gender or childhood or career or station in life, you can achieve a greater level of success.

I'm going to teach you how. This book is a step-by-step, turn-by-turn road map to your dream life. I will show you the right way to get started, the only way to get past the different roadblocks and obstacles you will encounter on your path, and the best way to balance life-changing productivity toward your goals while maintaining life-giving self-care. If you are breathing, and if you are willing to put in the work to chase your best life, this book will show you how to get where you want to be.

WHERE IT STARTED

Throughout my childhood and adolescence, I loved playing sports. My all-time favorite was soccer, and the midfield position was my happy place. Basically, it was my job to move the ball to the feet of the team's forward players, who would shoot the goal. Whether I was sprinting from one end of the field to the other or throwing the ball back in bounds after it had bounced out, I was always fast, competitive, and committed. To use the sports vernacular, I left everything I had on the field.

Looking back, I was darn good at soccer. But I also realize that part of me knew being a midfielder meant that I could work hard toward the team's win without bearing the responsibility and pressure of putting up points. I had convinced myself that I was good but not good enough to score goals. Instead, I wrapped myself in my identity as a helper and passed the ball to someone else who could score—someone who had the confidence and skill to get us the win.

I never even asked myself if this was really the position I wanted to play. Somewhere along the way I chose to let my passions take a backseat to my fears, all the while telling myself that I was simply doing what was best for the team. By the time I graduated from high school, this decision to prioritize and value others' abilities over my own had carried over into every aspect of my life.

As I got older, even while I achieved what would have been called success, I never thought of myself as being naturally talented. My assumption was that there would always be someone better skilled who had more important things to say than I did, so I accepted my role as the hardworking sidekick. When presented with the opportunity to lead, I was unwilling—not because I couldn't be bothered but because I had already disqualified myself. No matter how much I excelled, I treated myself as being inferior to everyone else. That inferiority became almost comfortable for me.

Then one day, it wasn't. My marriage was in crisis. My business had stagnated, in spite of the fact that others around me were excelling. I felt like I was raising our two young sons on my own, and I didn't even know who I was anymore. To add insult to injury, I couldn't seem to get rid of the last bit of pregnancy weight, no matter how much I ran or watched my diet. I had hit rock bottom.

It was miserable, and for the first time ever in my adult life, the thought of staying stuck scared me more than my fear of failing. I didn't want to be miserable anymore, not for another day, and I was ready to do whatever it took to get to the next level.

Almost immediately, I realized I had no idea where to start. I knew I desperately wanted my relationships to improve, to reconnect with myself, to work through the roadblocks in my business, and to get rid of my mom tummy. But how? If it was possible to reach a new low, that was it for me—the moment it occurred to me that I didn't have the slightest clue how to get out of that pit. It brought me to my knees.

Thank God. My complete and utter desperation carried me to the foot of the cross, which I found in the spare closet in our guest bedroom. I turned that little space into a sanctuary, and there I cried out to God. At first I did a lot of talking, but slowly I learned to listen. The more I became aligned with the Holy Spirit, the better my outlook became. This radical shift in my mind-set gave way to a profound sense of clarity about who God had created me to be and for what purpose. That knowledge ignited a passion in me that led to the research and study that eventually became the foundation of the process I'm about to teach you.

When I say that this book will show you how to get where you want to be, I say it with confidence because I know it works. This is the set of steps that ushered me from rock bottom into my dream life. It transformed me into a champion bodybuilder, took my marriage to new heights, allowed me to retire myself and my husband before the age of thirty, and has earned me multiple millions of dollars. Since then, I've had the pleasure of coaching thousands of men and women toward the life of their dreams using this exact method. I can't wait to take this journey with you and watch you cross the finish line to your own goals.

Perhaps right now you're at your own rock bottom, as I was. Or maybe you're stuck playing the midfielder or sidekick in someone else's dream and feel ready to step into your own strengths in order to pursue your unique passions and purpose. Maybe you were told that you were too bossy, shy, loud, quiet, fat, or skinny to reach the life you're drawn to. You might have heard that you were not smart, pretty, or good enough. Whatever you have believed about yourself, wherever you are in your life today, none of it matters. None of it should be a death sentence for your dreams—not anymore.

THE ROAD TO EVERYTHING YOU'VE EVER WANTED

My work crafting the method I'm going to teach you in these pages is rooted in more than a decade of academic research, trial, and success. As a trained counselor with a master's degree in psychology, I have spent years studying people and what makes them tick. Even though I retired from that profession and went on to earn multiple millions as a network marketing entrepreneur, I've spent hours since hanging up my cap and gown researching new information about the brain, the human mind, and why people do what they do. Nearly every day I comb through the Scriptures for new insight into how God made each person by His own perfect design. All together, I've invested more than ten thousand hours into researching science, experience, and Scripture to create the best and most direct pathway your best life.

The more I studied, the more I began to see the same pattern emerge. Every bit of research, each case study I examined, every interview I conducted and Bible passage the Holy Spirit showed me all pointed to the same thing: there are really only three phases to achieving success. Not surprisingly, each of the phases corresponds to a different part of your makeup: mind, heart, body. Put together in sequence, I call them the Dream Life Pathway, and they make up the only way of leveling the playing field so that anyone and everyone can pursue and achieve the life they were created to live. If you're ready to get to the next level in your life, relationships, and business, this is the road that will take you there.

Are you ready?

You can begin the life-changing journey of building your dream from the ground up today. your first step is crucial: You must decide that you want more for your life and that you're willing to work for it, even if that work takes you out of your comfort zone. Your second step, choosing the map you will use to chart your path toward your dream life, is just as important.

You didn't pick up this book by chance. I believe God brought it into your hands for such a time as this (Esther 4:14), and if you will engage with it, if you will trust me, I know it will change your life. That may sound like a bold statement, like something hard to guarantee, but I have seen it work so many times that there is no doubt in my mind that what I'm going to teach you in this book can show you how to design, pursue, and attain the life you always dreamed of. If you're ready to dig in to your dreams, let's get started.

Your Dream Life Begins Today

First, take a deep breath (through your nose, please), hold it for five seconds, open your mouth, and exhale. Now get comfortable and let go of any mental clutter. I want you to do this every time you sit down to read this book. When you are serious about making a change, making the time and space for change is crucial, and that time and space are sacred. This little ritual will help you transition from the goings-on of your daily life to the atmosphere in which you will create and then live your dream life.

Next, please do two quick things, if you haven't done them already:

- Grab a pen and something to sip on and find a comfortable spot.

- Make the commitment, right now, to complete every exercise laid out in these pages.

This isn't going to be a dry presentation of theory. Your work toward your dream begins here, on these pages. Reading these chapters without answering the questions will give you information but not the results that are possible when you read *and* act. To see real results, you will have to be intentional and engage with these exercises mentally, emotionally, and on paper. Furthermore, you cannot expect to achieve results if you skip the first phase and go right to the second or the third. Approach this pathway start to finish, and give it your full investment of energy and attention; resist the urge to complete chapters and their questions quickly.

I can promise you this: putting in the work is worth it. There is no shortcut to transformation, and questions like the ones in this book will help you learn more about yourself and about what you need to move forward. The work is always key. If this were a book on dieting, you would read the book, gather the recipes, and make a plan to incorporate the diet into your everyday life. You would consciously create new habits with the goal of developing a new life-style in order to see life-changing results. Approach this book the same way. Think of the exercises as new recipes to try. Give yourself the time and mental space to sit with each one. Then implement any new habits, ideas, or insights that come to you throughout the process.

This book is going to go deep, but my podcast, *Dream Cast*, and Facebook accountability group I actively mentor go even deeper. To get plugged in to these resources and access even more free tools to help you succeed, go to DeniseWalsh.com and join my e-mail list. From here on, we are on this journey together, and this is the easiest way we can remain in touch.

INNER REFLECTION:

Your Starting Place

Before you can move forward, you need a clear sense of where you are *now*. A simple review through the questions below will help you establish your starting place. In the coming months, you can look back at your answers to see how much progress you made and how much your life changed.

1. Describe your life situation, including your health, relationships, career, and overall satisfaction, as of today.

_____

_____

_____

_____

_____

_____

_____

_____

2. On a scale of one to ten (with ten being the most positive rating), what are your levels of joy, peace, and happiness in each of the following seven categories?

Family   1 2 3 4 5 6 7 8 9 10

Friendships   1 2 3 4 5 6 7 8 9 10

Finances   1 2 3 4 5 6 7 8 9 10

Health   1 2 3 4 5 6 7 8 9 10

Hobbies   1 2 3 4 5 6 7 8 9 10

Business   1 2 3 4 5 6 7 8 9 10

Giving back   1 2 3 4 5 6 7 8 9 10

3. Name three important people in your life. On a scale of one to ten, rate the quality of each relationship.

Name _____ 1 2 3 4 5 6 7 8 9 10

Name _____ 1 2 3 4 5 6 7 8 9 10

Name _____ 1 2 3 4 5 6 7 8 9 10

4. What do you hope to experience as you undertake this process and complete this workbook?

_____

_____

_____

_____

_____

5. What changes would you like to see in yourself and your life situation as a result of
   completing this workbook?

_____

_____

_____

_____

_____

6. Please attest to your answers with your signature and today's date below.

Sign _____

Date _____

Well done! You have a working baseline from
which to move forward. Now let's begin designing
your dream life.

PHASE #1

Shift Your Mind-set

one

Thoughts Matter—a Lot!

*Watch your thoughts, they become words; watch your
words, they become actions; watch your actions, they
become habits; watch your habits, they become character;
watch your character, for it becomes your destiny.*[1]

—Frank Outlaw

When you are charting the course toward your future—
when what's at stake isn't a matter of showing up to a
dinner party on time but arriving at your very destiny—
you need to take the most direct route, the first time. The voice you
tune in to for direction matters, and there is perhaps no louder or
more consistent voice in your life than the one inside your own head.
That's why before we can dive in to the nuts-and-bolts process of
identifying your passions, giving voice to your dreams, articulating
clear goals, and then taking empowered action, we have to start here,
with your thought life.

I know this isn't exactly the sexiest place to start. I can even
acknowledge that if you don't know me well, this might sound a lot
like the bland axioms I referred to in the introduction. But I need
you to trust me and hear me out when I say this step isn't about
learning to see the glass half full. I didn't do more than a decade
of research and coaching just to give you a pep talk about keeping

your chin up and staying optimistic. The truth is, the life you lead today and will lead in the future is determined by your thought life. Your success depends on it because what you think *produces* your future.

You can dream and plan and act until you are exhausted emotionally and physically, but you will never reach the life you've hoped for until you align yourself in such a way that you are in total control of the instructions your mind is giving to your body at all times. All that planning and action will help you develop a road map, sure. But this essential mind-set work we are about to do together will ensure you choose the most direct path, weather the inevitable storms, and navigate around the pitfalls that take others out of commission. It is what ensures your success this time around. It is what will make all the difference.

It isn't enough to be a positive person. You must learn to think and *be*, here and now, as you will think and be when you are living your best life. This *being* must proceed *doing*; it's more important. This is the God-given order of things. If you're ready to move your dream from your head to your heart to your life, we have to start in your mind.

THINK ABOUT YOUR THOUGHTS

The social sciences teach us that life is a series of actions and responses and that thinking precedes both. In other words, before every word you speak, before any action you take, during each reaction to the world and relationships around you, your brain is engaged in thought. Human beings average sixty thousand thoughts every single day. Ninety-five percent of these thoughts are habitual, being repeated over and over again. Here's the kicker: 80 percent of habitual thoughts are negative,[2] and because we hear them so often, they negatively influence our actions and responses to the world around us. Put simply, your negative thoughts and beliefs are taking a tremendous toll on you.

The effect of these thoughts isn't just purely mental. Our thoughts also affect us physiologically. Neuroscience explains how our thoughts affect the signals that are sent between our neurons to create thought paths. These thought paths eventually become our habits and beliefs, impacting our views of self and the world and influencing the way we treat others. According to the law attributed to neuropsychologist Dr. Donald Hebb, "Neurons that fire together, wire together."[3] In other words, habitual thoughts become part of our brain structure.

We will talk more about this later in greater detail, but here's a quick example: Think of someone who hurt you in some way. When you see their name or their face, what thoughts and emotions rise to the surface? Unless you've dealt with the pain, or possibly even trauma, they caused you, you're likely to go down the rabbit trial of negative thinking. "I don't like them." "They are mean." "Why does he get everything, even though he hurt me?" "If people knew what she did to me, they would act differently toward her." Because these thoughts are paired to the trigger, the person who hurt you, you simply see the trigger and suddenly experience a wave of emotions and negativity, and your thoughts are derailed for hours and maybe days.

But it doesn't have to be this way forever. Remember why you chose this workbook: you are ready for a change. To paraphrase Albert Einstein, "You cannot solve your problems with the same thinking that created them."[4] Even if you are unclear about exactly what sort of change you're looking for, if you want your life to look different, that difference begins with identifying and changing negative thought patterns. Job one as you begin your journey toward your dreams is to become consciously aware of your thoughts so you can identify patterns of thinking and their effect on the conduct of your life.

This is going to mean training yourself to be more aware of your thought life. For most, this is harder than it sounds. Being objective about other people's issues is easier than being objective about our own. For example, you can probably identify two groups of people whose thought habits are obvious to you. First are the people who live, eat, and breathe negativity. Whatever the day, they find ways to complain, believing that everything that can go wrong will go wrong. The second group are the people you'd rather be around. They are full of life, always positive, and convinced that goodness surrounds them.

The "dark cloud" people probably don't see themselves as being particularly negative. They are more likely to offer rationales for their point of view. They might even suggest that the upbeat crowd are luckier than they are, and probably unfairly so. But is that generalization accurate? Or might the people in each group be predisposed to certain outcomes because of their internal mind-sets? Let's find out.

HEAR, LISTEN, OBEY

In ancient Hebrew, the language in which much of the Bible was first recorded, there's a word—*shama'*—that has a lot to teach us about this issue of influence and the power we give to the voices we allow to speak into our lives. It shows up a lot in the Scriptures, but perhaps the most famous passage in which it appears is Deuteronomy 6:4–9:

> *Hear*, O Israel: The LORD our God, the LORD is one. Love the LORD your God with all your heart and with all your soul and with all your strength. These commandments that I give you today are to be on your hearts. Impress them on your children. Talk about them when you sit at home and when you walk along the road, when you lie down and when you get up. Tie them as symbols on your hands and bind them on your foreheads. Write them on the doorframes of your houses and on your gates. (emphasis added)

This passage is actually called "The Shema" after this word, which is translated "hear" at the start of verse 4. But that translation only scratches the surface of its full meaning. *Shama*ʿ actually means "to hear," "to listen...to consent, agree...yield to," and "to obey, be obedient."[5] This is interesting, because in English hearing, listening, agreeing, and obeying are four separate steps. Hearing is a passive exercise. You can hear something without tuning in to the sound or message. Listening is more active, but it's possible to listen without agreeing. Likewise, you can agree with a message and still choose not to take physical action to obey it. But with *shama*ʿ, the words we hear, however passively we absorb them, have an automatic and simultaneous effect on our actions, existence, and life itself.

This means that you can't just write off negative thoughts as background noise. Whether or not you are conscious of it, your inner monologue is shaping your view of yourself and your future. Your thoughts are building your destiny, for better or for worse, because what you hear directly impacts what you do. What you tell yourself matters because it manifests in your life.

I learned this the hard way. Years ago I was unhappy in my job as a clinical psychologist and knew I wanted a change, but I didn't know how to go about it. I was terrified to make the wrong move, so I did nothing. Plus, as I confessed in the introduction, my default was to assume my lot in life was to be a support player instead of a leader anyway. I waited for someone else to tell me what to do instead of taking empowered action myself. With these fears and self-limiting beliefs on replay inside my mind, I did nothing but stay unhappy. I was locked in a cycle of hearing the damning voice of my inner monologue, giving it my attention and consent, and allowing it to impact my actions. As a result, I stayed stuck way too long.

Eventually, I realized that the change I craved had to come from the inside out. Instead of allowing negative self-talk and worry to fill my head, I worked on shifting my thought life. I made a conscious decision not even to allow myself to hear the voice of my fears and insecurities. My dream life began the moment I chose only to listen to, agree to, and obey words of truth in agreement with my God-given purpose and destiny.

Your thought life will either be your most formidable obstacle or your greatest strength. It will impact your potential for success more than almost any other factor. This is not another limp, ambiguous piece of advice. It is actual science.

THINKING AND BEHAVIOR

Since the 1980s, Dr. Caroline Leaf has studied the mind–brain connection. Through her research and international clinical work, she developed the Geodesic Learning theory. Along with her colleagues Brenda Louw and Isabel Uys of the University of Pretoria in South Africa, they have explained the connections between internal thought processes and external outcomes.[6]

Merriam-Webster defines the word *geodesic* as "the shortest line between two points that lies in a given surface."[7] When applied to the curved surfaces and neural connections formed in the brain, this suggests two possibilities:

1. Our brains are lazy. When a decision needs to be made, the brain chooses the shortest possible neural connection that can process the circumstances without using more energy than necessary.

2. We create thousands, if not millions, of ingrained connections over the course of our lives. From these thinking patterns, we derive basic assumptions about ourselves and our world according to our life experiences, environment, and upbringing.

This tells us we make decisions habitually, via neurological shortcuts. Nine times out of ten, we end up picking the option that seems most obvious, even if it's not the best one. The same is true of our thoughts, which of course, go on to impact what we say, believe, and do. Over time, the pathways created by these habitual thoughts train us. Even though individual thoughts come and go quickly, they have a lasting impact on our self-image, behavior, relationships, and overall life experience. Our thoughts "train us."

Getting back to the example of negative and positive thinkers, the toxic thinking of your negative friends produces toxic outcomes and behaviors, among them, more hostile tones of voice and tense body language. Because their thoughts are negative, it is hard for them to identify or work around their counterproductive decisions, which were inspired by negative thought patterns in the first place.

The reverse is true for your upbeat friends. Their positive thoughts produce positive behaviors and communications, perpetuating cycles of positive thinking and doing. Their body language is more open, and their voices are more inviting. Because human beings are more perceptive in this state of mind, people in the positive crowd can more easily identify beneficial opportunities and are prone to making better decisions. This includes noticing and adjusting their thought habits to change future behavior.[8]

This is personal and very real to me. As I mentioned earlier, I spent years of my life waiting for something to change. I existed, almost mindlessly allowing my life and thoughts to happen *to* me. My thoughts said very negative things, which I came to believe.

"I don't have much value to add."

"I am not good enough."

"Who would want to listen to me?"

With these thoughts ruling over me, I never tried to score a goal on the soccer field. Instead, I stayed in the background, watching other players score. This belief system affected more than my athletic career. My teenage habit of passing the soccer ball morphed into an adult habit of letting opportunities pass me by.

Sometimes our habitual thoughts are simply untrue, and often they no longer point to who we want to be. In my case, I realized that I wasn't satisfied with just being a hard worker. As an adult, people weren't going to keep telling me what to do and what action to take. I had to take responsibility myself. When I eventually decided that if I wanted something different out of life, I would have to do something differently, my days of being a wallflower were over. I had something to say and value to add. I had learned to notice and question my habitual thoughts. Once that happened, change was possible! It is for you too.

Ingrained
Beliefs

INNER REFLECTION:

If you didn't already take the baseline assessment at the end of the introduction, take a moment to go back and do that right now. It contains some essential questions that will help you begin to engage with your own thought life, and it will give you a definitive starting point by which to measure any and all future progress. So flip back a few pages, fill it out, and then come back.

Back? Great! Let's keep going. As we discussed, your ingrained beliefs shape your world, just as my thinking shaped mine. The exercises at the end of this chapter will help you to notice your thoughts and beliefs and put them into words. Knowing what you're thinking is the first step. Then you can change those thoughts— and change your life.

As you explore your way of seeing life, notice the memories and experiences that pop up. Take your time responding to each question. Be sure to write down your full answers in these and all exercises. Writing causes you to think more deeply. The simple act of writing out your thoughts makes you more aware and better equipped to master them.

Finally, be thoughtful and transparent, remembering that there are no right answers, only truthful ones.

1. How do you view the world? Is it a friendly or unfriendly place? How do you believe the world sees you?

_____

_____

_____

_____

_____

2. Do you ever withhold your opinion or point of view when you really want to express it? How often, and why?

_____

_____

_____

_____

_____

3. What thoughts or concerns are with you habitually/daily (e.g., regarding finances, career, family, health and well-being, education, etc.)?

_____

_____

_____

_____

_____

_____

4. What ideas, beliefs, or concepts imparted
   to you during childhood are impacting you
   today? How are they evident in your life?

_____

_____

_____

_____

_____

Two

REPROGRAM YOUR BRAIN FOR SUCCESS

As [a man] thinks in his heart, so is he.

—PROVERBS 23:7, NKJV

THE BUILDING OF healthy thought habits is not about muttering, "I'm happy, I'm happy, I'm happy," and expecting your mood to brighten in an instant. It's about more than positive psychology, feel-good sayings, or repetitive-thinking exercises. What we are talking about here is making actual, structural changes to your brain.

Remember the work of Dr. Leaf and others from chapter 1, which showed how our thinking physically changes the brain's neural connections? The exciting truth is, if you can wire your brain toward the negative, then you can rewire it, no matter how long the self-limiting thought patterns and beliefs have been there. When you practice thinking in new ways, the wiring gets updated, regardless of your age or mental state. Your brain cells actually respond to changes in your thinking by rearranging themselves and creating more efficient thought patterns. This process is called neuroplasticity, a term derived from *neuron* "('pertaining to nerves'), and *plasticity*—meaning the ability of something to be molded or changed."[9] Because of this neuroplasticity, the brain can be rewired again and again.

This means you can literally mold your mind to become happier, more positive, more productive, or more of whatever you desire. You are not stuck forever with the thoughts, feelings, attitudes, and behaviors you experience now. Your mind-sets are not set in stone. By intentionally exercising gratitude, prayer, and meditation, you can dismantle any negative, self-sabotaging thought habits and alter the structure of your brain to develop patterns of positive, self-empowering thought.[10] In fact, you'll be able to start doing this by the end of this chapter.

OWNING IT

Taking a self-empowering approach is a mind-set all by itself. It is the complete opposite of victim thinking, which makes us out to be helpless recipients of life's circumstances. The more empowering approach allows us to recapture our God-given power with an abundance mind-set that is anything but passive.

Jack Canfield, the best-selling author of *Chicken Soup for the Soul*, writes about how to do this in his book *The Success Principles*. The book's first principle is incredibly simple yet powerful: you can take back your power by taking 100 percent responsibility for your life.[11] This means acknowledging that you *can* control your finances, relationships, career, and inner thoughts—and then actually do it. He says in order to succeed at changing your thought life, you need to recognize and replace three common thought habits: blaming, complaining, and making excuses. Canfield talks about them in regard to taking responsibility because they are three of the most negative habits and the most damaging.[12] We need to talk about them too.

Blaming

When you are running late for an appointment, the easiest "out" is to blame traffic. When you feel overworked, a typical response is to blame your boss. Shifting blame is a convenient way to excuse your feelings and your own failure to change. But the longer you do it, the longer you stay stuck, because blaming others gives them your power. Rather than seeing yourself as someone who overcomes obstacles, you assume the identity of a victim, a helpless recipient of another person's wrongdoing. It's an easy trap to fall into, but it will cost you more than you bargained to lose.

The brain's response to blaming can be explained with the Geodesic Learning theory discussed in chapter 1.[13] The neural connection that identifies a person or thing as the source of our problems is shorter and requires less energy than the connection we make when we consider the full range of factors that lead to a negative outcome, including the possibility that we contributed to it. That neural shortcut focuses on a convenient person or object on which to hang the blame and ignores other essential information. This short-circuits the opportunity for growth, supports a false perception of the issue, and obscures the course corrections that could produce better future outcomes.

Complaining

Not long ago, my husband, Brandon, and I visited my ninety-five-year-old great-aunt Beth, who lives states away from us. I had not seen my aunt in more than twenty years, but she was still as sharp as a tack. What a special visit it was! We shared sweet memories over lunch and even talked about world events. Then I asked Aunt Beth to give me some general advice for living. She thought about it for a few minutes and said, "Don't tell everyone all of your problems. No one really cares!" Brandon and I looked at each other and laughed. Aunt Beth was absolutely right!

We often complain to people who cannot solve our problems. We call it *venting*, but it's run-of-the-mill whining. It does nothing more than draw attention to the emotions and experiences from which we say we want to be free.

Is complaining one of your go-to thought habits? How many times have you complained (or dare I say, gossiped) to someone only to regret it the next day? Have you dumped your marriage complaints on your coworkers or burdened your carpooling passengers with road rage rants because someone cut you off? What did your unloading accomplish? Was letting off some steam worth it?

Even if you are already curbing your complaining, you can probably remember a time when airing your complaints felt really good. If you're honest with yourself, you know that under the right conditions, complaining could rear its ugly head again.

When you feel the urge to complain, shift your focus. Instead of strengthening negative thought patterns, making those negative emotions stronger and more persistent, flip the script and try to find something positive in the situation. In doing so, you'll rewire your brain, and before long, you'll find you attract positivity like a magnet.

Making excuses

Have you noticed that you consistently make time for what's important to you? There are only so many hours in a day, and you are only one person—the one person who decides which events you will attend, which ones you will miss, and which activities you will postpone.

Excuse-making has its own language. We say things like, "I don't have time for the gym," or, "I'm sorry I missed seeing you. I've been super busy." The truth is that we make time for the events and activities we intentionally prioritize. Everything else waits. I'm not suggesting that we have to say *yes* to everything. I'm simply encouraging some inner truth-telling about what we *cannot* do and what we *choose* not to do.

The sooner we understand how we capitulate to these tactics, the sooner we can free ourselves, take responsibility, and improve our lives. I'm not saying it's easy. Anytime you choose to change, you will encounter headwinds.

When I first learned these concepts, I wracked my brain to find ways around them. I simply could not imagine handling my problems without blaming, complaining, and making excuses. A particular argument I had with myself stands out. I was driving through at least a foot of snow in the thick of the Michigan winter while listening to *The Success Principles* on audiobook. Annoyed by the snow, I told myself (and Jack Canfield, for that matter), "I don't have control over the weather, so I'm allowed to complain about it!" The idea made sense to me: If I could change the weather, I would have done it. If I had that power and chose not to use it, then my complaints would be disqualified. But I didn't have that power, so I was in the clear.

Deep down, I seemed to hear Canfield shooting my argument full of holes. It was my own conscience calling me out and saying, "Denise, you chose to live in Michigan." I thought, "Crap! It's true!" Technically, I could have moved to Florida or Southern California. But I didn't. I chose to live in a place where snow falls up to six months out of twelve.

Then I dug for more clever rationales. "Yes, but I couldn't move to a warm, sunny state because it would be too expensive. And I should live closer to my parents anyway." Even these ideas fell flat as I thought them. The truth was that if I *really* hated snow, I could find a way to move. Where I lived *was* under my control. Therefore, I had no right to complain. As if I needed any more evidence, I realized that I almost never complained about the things I couldn't change. I just accepted them and moved on.

Accepting the truth about my thought games was not an attractive idea at first, but I worked at it. I backslid plenty of times, but I eventually surrendered them. I knew that taking full responsibility for my life—including my thought life—was the only route to a better future. Putting in the work to shift your mind-set will do the same for you.

ANCIENT WISDOM, MODERN APPLICATIONS

If we can change our thoughts, we can change everything that follows: our communication, behavior, relationships, and more. This is not pop psychology; it is the way we were created. The Bible teaches us to control our thoughts and focus on life-affirming ones, as the following Scriptures show:

> We demolish arguments and every pretension that sets itself up against the knowledge of God, and we take captive every thought to make it obedient to Christ.
>
> —2 CORINTHIANS 10:5

> Death and life are in the power of the tongue, and those who love it will eat its fruit.
>
> —PROVERBS 18:21, NASU

> Do not conform to the pattern of this world, but be transformed by the renewing of your mind. Then you will be able to test and approve what God's will is—his good, pleasing and perfect will.
>
> —ROMANS 12:2

These truths address the power of our thoughts and words in shaping our character. It might seem perfectly normal to go to bed stressed out and awaken the same way, but Proverbs 23:7 shows that we can choose what to think and how to feel. The Bible teaches that we should be conscious and in control of our thoughts, renewing them so we can be changed. Clearing out old, limiting thought habits allows us to more easily recognize God's will and become our supernatural selves. By governing our thoughts, we can transform and transcend our old patterns and live the way the Holy Spirit calls us to live.

Let's start by becoming more aware of what we're thinking so that we can intentionally take our thoughts captive. The exercises below will help you pinpoint your current thought habits and make positive changes. After you complete the exercises, I encourage you to revisit them as new challenges arise in your thought life.

Changing your Thought Habits

INNER REFLECTION:

Changing your life means being aware and open to altering your thinking. The only way to stop blaming, complaining, and making excuses is to become good at catching yourself in the act. So, step one is awareness. Step two is to replace negative mind-sets with more positive ones.

As you answer the questions below, be thoughtful and dig deep. Remember, don't search for the right answers. Just be real about working through your issues and getting free from victim mind-sets.

1. What complaints do you make on a regular basis?

_____

_____

_____

_____

_____

2. On what or whom do you tend to pin blame for your situations and challenges?

_____

_____

_____

_____

_____

_____

3. What are your go-to excuses?

_____

_____

_____

_____

Next, you will practice taking full responsibility for your life and outcomes. The following questions are tough. Reflect on them for as long as it takes to render an honest answer and challenge your habitual blaming, complaints, and excuses. Answer the questions with respect to a specific situation that triggered you to play the victim.

4. Describe the situation you faced.

_____

_____

_____

_____

5. What was your role, whether by action
   or inaction, in creating this situation or in
   allowing it to happen?

_____

_____

_____

_____

_____

_____

_____

6. Describe what you really want in regard to
   this situation.

_____

_____

_____

_____

7. What changes will you make in order to
   attain what you really want?

_____

_____

_____

_____

_____

_____

Now let's reflect on your reflections. There's a world of difference between identifying what can be changed and accepting what is out of your control. Alcoholics Anonymous has mastered this distinction. They sum it up with an excerpt from Reinhold Niebuhr's "Serenity Prayer": "God, grant me the serenity to accept the things I cannot change, courage to change the things I can, and the wisdom to know the difference."[14]

The point of the above exercises was to act out this prayer by identifying three things:

1. your role in a real-life situation,
2. what you really want to see happen, and
3. what changes are possible for you to make.

When this kind of awareness becomes habitual, you become proactive rather than reactive.

If this still feels counterintuitive, that's OK. That's only because it is! It probably won't feel normal at first, but doing things you have never done is the only way to have a life you have never had. Remember the Geodesic Learning theory: the human mind seeks shortcuts. So its default is to deflect, disassociate, move on, and adapt to the status quo. This might be natural, but if you really want to create your best life, you must tap into your supernatural self. It is the overcoming side of you that chooses to take responsibility. You cannot

solve your problems using the same thinking that created them.

God has imbued you with the power to live your fullest
life, and that life starts inside your thoughts. Your first
priority must be to become more self-aware and intentional in your thinking. Don't let your mind run away with
you. Harness your thoughts and their power. Take them
captive, as the Scriptures command. These questions
will help:

8. What was your first waking thought this
   morning?

_____

_____

9. What do you typically think about before
   bedtime?

_____

_____

_____

_____

_____

Now that you have a sense of your typical morning
and nighttime thoughts, let's initiate new, intentional
thought patterns.

When you see each day as a great day, you will
take it on optimistically, knowing that good things can

happen. You'll keep your eyes peeled for them! Instead of dreading the day and "waiting for the other shoe to drop," you will believe that, even if you don't get your way today, things will work out for your benefit in the end.

Below is a list of new thoughts to start the morning. Consider what each statement implies. Then adopt each statement as it is, revise it, or let it inspire your own thoughts.

Today is a great day.

I love my life.

I am happy and grateful for my family.

I am happy and grateful for my current situation.

Thank You, God, for being with me today.

10. Now jot down some intentional morning thoughts of your own.

_____

_____

_____

_____

_____

Next, let's make a list of new thoughts to ponder before bedtime. Consider what each statement implies. Then adopt each as it is, revise it, or let it inspire your own thoughts.

Thank You, God, for an amazing day.

Thank You for the impact I made in the world today.

I love my life, and I know where I am going.

I am excited about what's in store tomorrow.

11. Add some bedtime thoughts of your own.

_____

_____

_____

_____

_____

12. Download the free list of Bible verses I put together for you at DeniseWalsh.com. Read over them often as constant reminders to think and speak powerful, positive thoughts that can change your life.

Now reconsider the following words from a new place of understanding:

Watch your thoughts, they become words; watch your words, they become actions; watch your actions, they become habits; watch your habits, they become character; watch your character, for it becomes your destiny.

Three

Awakened With Gratitude

Be thankful for what you have and you'll end up having more. If you concentrate on what you don't have, you will never, ever have enough.[15]

—Oprah Winfrey

THE EARLIEST VERSION of what we now call Murphy's Law said, "Anything that can happen, will happen given enough trials." Over time the axiom has evolved to say "Anything that can go wrong, will go wrong." This later meaning became popular with the military and stressed the need to prepare for all possible scenarios. Today, the saying has devolved into a favorite mantra of cynics. People with Murphy's Law stamped into their thinking wake up worried about every possible upset, disruption, and worst-case scenario. What else can you do when you believe that every negative outcome is headed your way? Your only hope is to hunt it down before it finds you! Sounds like fun, right?

Not really, but there is an alternative: You can wake up with the completely opposite outlook every single day. It proceeds from a grateful heart and comes in countless flavors. Here are two:

- Whatever can go right, will go right!

- I am always at the right place at the right time.

How different would life be with mottoes like that working for you? The answer is *very different*. When your outlook is fearful and you expect poor outcomes, you end up feeling sad, angry, and resentful. When your outlook is one of gratitude, you feel good about all you are and all you possess. You are attuned to the confirmations that pop up and reassure you. They remind you that you're moving in the right direction and your needs will be met at the right time. Your mind naturally opens up to encouraging thoughts and the pervasive sense that life is good.

Why is that? The branch of physics known as quantum physics sheds light on how your thoughts impact everything you experience.[16] I mention it because it provides some understanding of the types of energy your thoughts produce. Quantum physics and classical physics are not the same. The father of classical physics is Sir Isaac Newton. The discipline he initiated deals with certainty in terms of what we physically see and experience. For example, if I throw a rock into a pond, I can predict the size of the ripples based on the weight of the rock and the speed at which it travels. Classical physicists see matter and energy as existing separately, so that the rock and the energy I use to throw the rock are separate.

Quantum physics explores what is uncertain even with scientific observation and theorizes that energy and matter are less distinct and more connected than traditional physicists thought. Powerful magnification tools reveal, for example, that the atom is not solid. It is a tiny force field of energy created by smaller particles spinning at incredible rates of speed. The energy created by a single atom works with the energy created by millions, billions, or trillions of other atoms to produce the physical world we see.

Energy can take many forms. We can absolutely feel other people's emotional energy, just as they feel ours. Like human transmission towers, we broadcast our internal world through the emotional energy we release into the external world. That energy has an effect. Think about how the atmosphere changes when an angry person enters a room. Everyone is affected! A positive, high-energy person can also own the space within moments, but in a more uplifting manner.

Apply this understanding of emotional energy to the person you are right now and the person you are becoming. Every particle of your being has the potential to renew itself. In this dynamic setting, every moment becomes an opportunity. Every interaction offers something new. You can direct your energy, including your thoughts, in any direction you choose. Your selected thoughts produce corresponding actions, which you see as being either positive or negative (which happen to be energy terms).

That's the theoretical side of thought energy. Next, let's dive into the practical aspects of using positive thoughts to shape your dream life.

TAKING THE HIGH ROAD

What do you suppose is the most powerful form of thought energy? Is it anger? Determination? Problem-solving? The Bible speaks of the power of love, saying, "Now these three remain: faith, hope and love. But the greatest of these is love" (1 Cor. 13:13). In terms of our thought life, love takes many forms. In terms of transforming us, I believe that gratitude is love's most powerful manifestation. When we are feeling truly thankful, the energy that love produces fills us up inside.

The Bible connects gratitude to our receiving of God's love. For example, Psalm 9:1 says, "I will *give thanks* to you, LORD, with all my heart; I will tell of all your wonderful deeds" (emphasis added). Philippians 4:6-7 says, "Do not be anxious about anything, but in every situation, by prayer and petition, *with thanksgiving*, present your requests to God. And the peace of God, which transcends all understanding, will guard your hearts and your minds in Christ Jesus" (emphasis added).

Love, gratitude, and appreciation are the highest of all emotional states—that is, they have a higher vibrational energy than negative emotions, like anger and jealousy—and they powerfully raise our emotional energy. When we tune in to the high-frequency emotion of gratitude, we bathe others in joy, possibility, hope, and peace. This unlocks our connection to them and to the Divine, and it opens our hearts to receive even more positive energy. We become like magnets, attracting blessings and repelling curses.

Low-vibrational emotions such as guilt and shame work the opposite way, keeping us stuck in states of emotional paralysis and suffering. We don't have to stay there! When we shift from low-frequency thoughts to high-frequency ones, we trigger the domino effect that shifts our circumstances and improves our sense of well-being.

Canfield explains that in the realm of thought energy, "like attracts like."[17] When you adopt an attitude of gratitude, "you will naturally attract more for which you can be grateful."[18] I'm talking about a focused and almost explosive gratitude that reaches beyond simple thank yous and appreciative smiles. This type of gratitude leaps from your heart with excitement and force. As this practice becomes lifestyle, it cause shifts in outlook and create entry points for new blessings to pour in![19]

Retraining your brain to create new neuropathways and thought patterns begins with recognizing the good in your life, which rewires your nervous system and literally changes your brain chemistry.[20] When you upgrade your emotional energy to the level of gratitude and love, you draw into your life what comes less easily when you are in an emotional down state. Suddenly, the right people and opportunities cross your path, because you are better able to connect with them.

People who express gratitude aren't just happier or more successful. They are healthier, better equipped to face challenges, and have stronger relationships too.[21] Can you see why it is so crucial to rewire your brain?

ENJOY THE PROCESS

Are you ready for one more important mind-set shift? This was a tough one for me to learn, but it was worth it. It involves being present to the moment, enjoying the journey, and valuing the time spent on a given task.

One of my favorite sayings is, "I love where I am, and I know where I am going." To put it another way, "I love who I am, and I know who I am becoming." For an achiever personality like mine, loving where I am takes some doing. My natural default is to focus on future goals. My eyes always wander to the finish line, because getting the win is so much fun.

My achiever's perspective has a definite downside. *Someday* is always out there, yet always hanging over my head. Plus, the satisfaction of the win is always in the future. That leaves little appreciation for the process. I confess I am not a process person *at all*! I just love checking stuff off my list. Even if the finish isn't perfect, I can say, "I'm done!" (Yes, I have even been known to add tasks I have already completed to my to-do list, just so I can cross them off. It's kind of an obsession with me.) Through trial and error and lots of hiccups, I have discovered the fallacy of my approach: the so-called finish line never comes—and for good reason! Once I hit a goal, I always choose a new one. My life is a race that never ends!

Can you relate? Does it seem that as soon as you check off one project, a new one demands your attention? Of course it does! That is the reality of life. What matters is how you view the continuum. I realize now that the process is as precious as the completion. Living in the moment makes life work so much better. It took some time, but I learned that when my only focus was on the finish line, enjoyment was scarce, I tired more easily, and my attitude turned sour.

That is counterproductive! Work is a lot harder when you are negative. You cannot be grateful when "getting it done" is uppermost in your mind. Being overly focused on the finish is a deception. It says that the achievement—the new car, the new job, the new house, or whatever—will give you the peace you long for. What a trap that is! It means you cannot enjoy your life until you fulfill a certain goal; and because life is a series of goals, enjoyment is permanently postponed. Grouchiness becomes your new normal, and you are blinded to the moment you are in, literally.

In June 2009, *The Journal of Neuroscience* published a study proving that a bad mood—the emission of unhappy frequencies—compromises the brain's processing of information and impacts the visual cortex, which is the part of the brain responsible for sight. However, happy test subjects found 50 percent more of what they were looking for on a visual search-and-find activity, compared with their unhappy counterparts.[22] A bad mood can actually impair your vision, while a good mood enhances your field of view. I see this as groundbreaking information that should motivate all of us to cure our bad moods once and for all.

That's where the first part of my motto comes in: "I love where I am, and I know where I am going." Loving where you are is the primary lesson I hope you'll take from this chapter. By choosing to enjoy where and who you are *today*, you'll be able to embrace the journey toward your dreams and the process of transformation. When you value the journey as much as the finish line, you will be infinitely happier and more excited about moving forward.

I can testify to this truth! My life is so much richer when I am focusing on the people I love and the things that are happening right now. Thankfully (pun intended), living on the gratitude frequency is something we can all do, just by tuning in. Yes, it takes practice. All good things do. The payoff is so worth it, however. Not only will your *now* be more enjoyable, but you will receive more of what you want in the future.

Gratitude Transcends Your Circumstances

Remember that we're talking about intense gratitude, not easy thank yous to the people with whom you interact each day. This gratitude is excited and emotionally connected. It causes you to love where you are, even though the bills keep coming, there's turmoil at home, and you are expecting a potentially serious call from your doctor. Explosive gratitude helps you to focus on the positives and the goodness around you and within you. It is your self-generated source of energy, whenever you need it.

Gratitude is mentioned all through the Bible. These are a couple of my favorite mentions:

> In everything give thanks. For this is God's will for you in Christ Jesus.
> —1 THESSALONIANS 5:18, NET

> Whatever is true, whatever is honorable, whatever is just, whatever is pure, whatever is lovely, whatever is commendable, if there is any excellence, if there is anything worthy of praise, think about these things.
> —PHILIPPIANS 4:8, ESV

It should be no surprise that gratitude is vitally connected to our faith. When you are focused on the problems around you, there is little opportunity to feel truly grateful for the blessings God has given to you. In fact, in terms of the vibrational energy of your emotions, it is impossible to be truly grateful and truly angry at the same time. As we saw before, this is just one way focusing on the negative can make it hard for you to attract and receive new blessings and solutions to the setbacks in your life.

Despite their devastating situations, even the blind, people with leprosy, and others had enough faith to come to Jesus *expecting* to be healed. They intentionally focused on what they wanted, thanked God before they received healing, and expected miracles to happen. And guess what? They did! The Bible shares thirty-one stories like this of Jesus healing the sick or dying.[23] One desperately ill woman believed she would be healed if she could only touch the hem of Jesus's garment. She touched it and was made whole. (See

Matthew 9:20–22.) In another daunting case, some men believed so strongly in Jesus's ability to heal the sick that they removed part of a rooftop and lowered their paralyzed friend to where Jesus was. Immediately, Jesus healed him. (See Luke 5:17–26.)

So many times we pray for God's help, but we don't pray specifically for the outcome we want. In other cases, we pray, but in the secret parts of our heart we don't really trust that God will do it, or that He won't do it *for us*. But with regard to at least one of His promises to us—to you—God says, "Test me now in this" (Mal. 3:10). Numbers 23:19 reminds us, "God is not human, that he should lie, not a human being, that he should change his mind. Does he speak and then not act? Does he promise and not fulfill?" Each of the thirty-one people who came to Jesus for healing trusted in His promises more than they trusted what they physically saw in front of them. They focused on what He could do instead of focusing on what they couldn't. Expect the outcome you want, focus your heart and spirit on it in faith, and trust that God will be faithful, even if you can't see the answer to your prayers yet.

PRACTICING GRATITUDE

When I began work on my master's degree at Wheaton College, my great-aunt and great-uncle took Brandon and me around the town to acquaint us with the area. I particularly remember the car ride we took that day. In fact, I'll never forget it. At every point along the way, Aunt Frances and Uncle Frank found something beautiful to admire.

"What a beautiful willow tree!" Aunt Frances exclaimed.

"It sure is a nice day," Uncle Frank replied.

Around every corner, they found more reasons to be grateful: the fall leaves, the new coffee shop, the young mother taking her baby for a walk. They did more than enjoy it for themselves; they verbalized their appreciation, which encouraged Brandon and me.

Throughout my college years, Brandon and I played a little

game with Aunt Frances and Uncle Frank. Teasing them, we verbally appreciated *everything*, no matter how silly it seemed. We said things like, "What fun the squirrels are having," or, "The clouds sure are beautiful." We really were jesting and the game did make us laugh, but it formed in us the habit of appreciating the little things.

If you're paying attention, a thousand things can make you thankful each day. I purposely appreciate the woods in my backyard. I give thanks for my mom, who lives close by. I am even thankful for the grocery store where I purchase my veggies. All of it keeps me actively grateful throughout the day. And why shouldn't I be? When God created the world, He said that it was good. So it's good!

You can agree with Him by speaking out your thankfulness. It might sound silly, but go ahead and try it. Then watch how your mood and your life improve!

What a Beautiful Life

INNER REFLECTION:

Take a mental snapshot of your life right now. Are you living in the spirit of fear and grouchiness or the spirit of gratitude? What does your daily, habitual attitude look like? Consider your current family, work, and health situation and intentionally notice what is already working in your favor. The following exercises will help you.

1. List ten beautiful things about your life.

_____   _____

_____   _____

_____   _____

_____   _____

_____   _____

2. Why are you grateful for these things?

_____

_____

_____

_____

3. Use the memory-joggers below by completing the sentences or filling in the blanks:

I am grateful for my family because

_____

_____

_____.

I am grateful for my friendship with

_____

because

_____

I am grateful for who I am because

_____

_____

_____.

What's something good that happened this week?

_____

_____

_____

_____

What's something silly for which you are grateful?

_____

_____

_____

_____

Name something else for which you are graeful.

_____

_____

_____

_____

4. In the table below, list ten people for whom
   you are explosively grateful and list one way
   to express your gratitude to each.

NAME	EXPRESSION OF GRATITUDE
_____	_____
_____	_____
_____	_____
_____	_____
_____	_____
_____	_____
_____	_____
_____	_____
_____	_____
_____	_____

5. Fill in the blank: When I flood my mind with
   thankfulness, I feel:

_____

_____

_____

_____.

6. Tweaking your thought habits can be fun. The following tips will help you become more consciously aware of your blessings as you incorporate gratefulness into your lifestyle.

- Pretend that you are on vacation every day. Think about how your view of the world and your interaction with people would change with a vacation outlook.

- Make time to appreciate everything you are, have, and do. Mentally articulate your joy in all of it.

- Appreciate others *deeply*. Develop a more conscious awareness of those around you—at the checkout counter, the mailbox, your children's school, and especially at home. Actively choose to *see* them and their inherent value as human beings.

7. Reminders, seen and read throughout the day, can reinforce your intention to be grateful, even when difficult situations distract and drain you. Set a timer on your phone to go off at regular intervals and prompt you to take a moment to be mindful of the good things happening in your life at that moment. The more conscious effort you put into learning this skill, the more natural it will become. As you create new thought paths, your ability to see, feel, and experience blessings will improve.

A word to the wise: these exercises are meant to be done every day. A once-in-a-while approach won't have the lasting impact you desire. Also, a grateful and abundant mind-set can be cultivated, but it probably won't come naturally. That's OK! It's a matter of working your gratitude "muscles" so they can create strong new thought patterns.

Big changes start with incremental shifts in direction. Over time, even small adjustments in your habitual patterns will produce radical change. Keep it up, and your new way of thinking will become your new way of life. From a place of lack, you can move toward abundance. From the place of sorrow and grief, you can move toward a life of joy, fulfillment, and peace. It happens one decision and one thought at a time.

Four

ALIGNMENT LEADS TO ACHIEVEMENT

Be still, and know that I am God.

—PSALM 46:10

OW LONG DO you think you could jog before your body wouldn't let you take another step? What about a sprint? I'm not talking about healthfully pushing yourself beyond the threshold of your current level of fitness. I'm talking about crossing that line and then continuing forward until your muscles seize and you fall head over feet. How far would you get? Beyond that, how long do you think it would take your body to recover afterward?

Most of us would never even consider trying this, and with good reason. The effects would be catastrophic and possibly even permanent. It is no way to treat the human body. And yet all day, nearly every day, to-do lists, schedules, appointments, dings, rings, and other electronic notifications keep us mentally jogging and sprinting from one thing to the next without pause. This relentless daily pace means that even when our minds are actively engaged with the task at hand, our brains and bodies have been conditioned to stay on full alert, anticipating our transition to one of the myriad other items on the docket. Too many of us start the day mentally at an all-out run and don't slow our pace until bedtime. If we think to pray, it is often fleeting. We thank God for our meal or for some unexpected blessing, and then we continue on at breakneck speed.

In modern society, we pat each other on the back for this sort of behavior. "Way to multitask!" we say encouragingly. To avoid being found lacking or slacking, we pound caffeinated drinks and high-sugar foods that carry us from energy high to energy high, and all in the name of keeping the plates spinning and crossing off the items on our agenda. We justify our decision not to prioritize prayer and silence because, well, where would we find the time?

If this is hitting home, let me speak bluntly: this pace is causing you harm—slowly, maybe, but surely—and stunting your ability to reach your dreams. That's because you cannot gain clarity about your goals or the best way of pursuing them without connectedness. Apart from the health benefits of meditation, tuning in to the voice of the Lord and tuning out the din of the world will expand your overall potential exponentially.

Mindfulness, Meditation, and Faith

For thousands of years the Bible has spoken of meditation and challenged believers to do it. Following are just a few examples of biblical meditation, as presented in both the Old and New Testaments of the Bible:

- King David focused on God's judgments and actions, saying, "I will *meditate* on Your precepts and regard Your ways" (Ps. 119:15, NASU, emphasis added).

- Joshua 1:8 commands us to "*meditate* on [the Bible] day and night so you will be sure to obey everything written in it" (NLT, emphasis added).

- The apostle Paul instructed Timothy to focus on God's Word, saying, "*Meditate* on these things; give yourself entirely to them, that your progress may be evident to all" (1 Tim. 4:15, NKJV, emphasis added).

When I talk about meditation and mindfulness, I'm referring to listening for His voice in His Word and through the promptings of His Holy Spirit, both during intentional, set-apart quiet time or during the course of your day. This creates the space for you to hear Him and experience what He is stirring up within you, and it will allow you to keep your mind and heart aligned with the Holy Spirit's direction for your life. Because it connects us to Him on a deeper level, this practice will help you to blossom into the person God created you to be.

Has an amazing idea ever come to mind during your morning shower or as you lay in bed at night? These are the types of experiences I began to enjoy every day almost as soon as I reprioritized to begin my day with dedicated time with God. As I learned to take my thoughts captive, I entered into a state of lower-range beta waves—more on this in a bit—which healed my mind, allowed me to repair my body, and created the mental space for me to listen. Soon, I began finding pieces of myself that I had lost. Passions and goals that I'd parked on the back burner returned to the front of my mind and stirred my heart. My purpose came into clear focus, and I was able to align my actions perfectly with my dreams and destiny. It was powerful and life-changing. It can be that way for you too.

THE SCIENCE OF PRAYER AND MEDITATION

We don't pray because of science. We pray because we believe and want to communicate with God, who loves us unconditionally and has a plan for our life. But science does confirm the life-giving benefits of prayer and meditation.

Dr. Leaf cites "over twelve hundred studies linking intentional prayer and overall health and longevity."[24] Research has found that twelve minutes of daily, focused prayer over a two-month period can alter the brain so significantly that the changes are visible and can be measured on a brain scan.[25] It also tells us that meditation can slow down our brain waves in ways that are beneficial to our immediate and long-term health.

Our everyday, conscious living takes place in one of three frequencies of those beta waves: low, mid, and high range.[26] Low-range beta waves occur when you are relaxed but interested. For example, reading a book draws your focus, lowers your attentiveness to other things, and relaxes your body. Mid-range beta waves indicate a more active state of attention, such as when you are learning or engaged in more analytical thinking. High-range beta waves are produced during more demanding and stressful situations. These are your brain's most engaged moments.

Like jogging or running to the point of muscle failure, extended periods of high-range beta waves can disorder the brain, with an unhealthy range of stress chemicals tipping it out of balance. For those who experience this state for extended periods, suffering (including increased anxiety, worry, anger, and pain) becomes the norm. An extreme example is post-traumatic stress disorder (PTSD), in which the body continues to react as though the stressful situation were still underway, even long after it has ended. The body was not built for this. As a habitual state it can be draining and cause all sorts of other problems. In addition to the physical impact, the constant emotional crisis fractures mental focus and scatters thought processes, so that learning becomes more difficult.

Overcoming this cycle of damaging high-range beta waves requires real changes in thought habits and in the brain itself. Meditation is a powerful tool in this regard. It addresses issues of extended or habitual stress and aids overall well-being by shifting brain waves to the low-range beta variety.[27] These lower ranges increase awareness, learning, and access to subconscious thinking.

Even a small amount of meditation each morning can have beneficial results throughout the rest of your day. In a study done at the University of Madison, the brain activity of Buddhist monks was monitored as they practiced their form of meditation each morning. The monks' brains were scanned again after a full day of normal activity. Even after exposure to the chaotic signals of the external world, brain scans showed that they maintained the low beta wave frequency they achieved during their morning meditation.[28] Clearly, when you begin your day by slowing down your brain, you can maintain a more serene state throughout the day.

This research is compelling, but my firsthand experience with the transformative power of prayer and meditation was enough to convince me to move it to the top of my priority list. These practices didn't just change me; they changed *everything*.

MY TRIP TO ROCK BOTTOM

Have you gone through something that shook you to your core, shifted the trajectory of your life, and set you on a totally unexpected path? In one way or another, most of us can say, "Yup, I've been there and done that." For me, it was hitting rock bottom in my personal life. My slide downhill began in 2014.

First, though, a little backstory. Growing up in a Methodist church in Troy, Michigan, deeply shaped my faith. I loved my church and felt very supported by the community of adults who loved and cared for me. Through years of youth groups, mission trips, serving in my community, and small group experiences, I learned what it meant to develop my relationship with God through prayer. That meant setting aside time to open my heart and align myself with Him.

Though what I learned was amazing, it was not complete. I thought my prayer life was supposed to help me feel good and be good. So I fired off quick prayers before meals and at bedtime. I thanked God for His blessings and told Him about my personal desires. I assumed that He heard me, but I was never certain that praying impacted my day-to-day life. If someone had asked me, I would have confidently asserted that I was in relationship with God, but truth be told, it was more like a silent partnership; I was neither listening nor speaking much.

This remained the status quo during crucial seasons of my life, like the transition from teenager to adult, high schooler to college grad, and single woman to wife. Let me tell you, with that last transition, I felt on top of the world. June 11, 2005, was the absolute best day of my life—the day I became Mrs. Denise Walsh. It wasn't hard to fall in love with Brandon. He was handsome, successful, fun, hardworking, athletic, and loving (and those are only some of his best qualities). My new husband embodied everything I had ever dreamed of and prayed for in a partner.

We dated for four years before we tied the knot. On our wedding day we were privileged to celebrate with our favorite people. Then we went off to Puerto Vallarta, Mexico, for our honeymoon and a blissful start of our life together. It was a solid beginning for our shared dreams and desires, mutual respect and understanding, and good, old-fashioned love.

Two years later we started our network marketing business together, which freed us to quit our full-time jobs and embark on whole new realms of adventure. Seven years after our wedding, our family started to grow, and by 2013, our family was double the size. Brandon and I were and are the proud parents of Owen and Eli, our two magnificent red-haired, bright-eyed boys.

Seemingly in the blink of an eye, our life had become *really* busy! Hustling to raise our children and build our individual and shared careers, we experienced what a lot of young married couples do: a gradual but noticeable loss of intimacy. Judging by appearances, our nuclear family was perfect. Yet an ever-present tension was creeping in, and Brandon and I were drifting apart. Before long, we hit a roadblock and got stuck there, each of us convinced that we were right and the other was wrong. The idea of compromise slipped more and more out of reach.

Marital bliss and mutual respect gave way to turmoil. I struggled to understand the decisions my husband—the one person I was supposed to know more intimately than any other—was making. Inside I was in knots, but on the outside I tried to keep the drama and stress levels down. So I walked on eggshells. The perfect dream life I envisioned and prayed for was dissolving into chaos, confusion, and uncertainty. Our shared life became two individual lives lived under one roof. At our lowest point, I felt like I was raising our two boys as a single parent.

UNEXPECTED BLESSING

During this tumultuous period, I realized there were three ways that I could deal with my problems. I could make changes and accept the risks that changes would bring, I could accept the new normal and try to find peace in it, or I could do nothing and stay miserable.

Making changes seemed impossible. I was convinced that asking, begging, and yelling for change would only create more problems and convince Brandon that leaving was his best option. On the other hand, doing nothing was not an option, because I didn't want to stay miserable. By a process of elimination, I chose to accept my lot and deal with it. I didn't want to stay, but I didn't want to leave, either. Acceptance meant living in a fog.

Just when I thought all of our options had been exhausted, something out of the blue happened: I watched a movie that gave me new hope. It was *War Room*, a Christian drama about a seemingly perfect family that seemed to have it all but was being torn apart from within.[29] The film changed my life. It portrays a Realtor named Elizabeth who suspects her husband of cheating on her during his busy travel schedule. Other issues complicate their already tenuous relationship, with Elizabeth and her husband disagreeing about helping out her parents financially. Tensions increase in the marriage, and the couple seems to argue over every little thing.

Elizabeth feels hopeless. On a routine visit with a client, she ends up venting her frustrations and fears to Miss Clara, a seasoned believer who offers her own response to chaos: *she prays.* Miss Clara prayed more than "thank You for this food" types of prayers. In her very own prayer room, which happened to be her bedroom closet, Miss Clara talked to God at a whole other level, reading her Bible, writing in her journal, and seeking God with her entire heart. She did more than ask Him for help; she aligned herself with His promises, asked for His healing and intervention, and called for His will to be done in her life. As she does for Elizabeth in the movie, Miss Clara became for me an inspiring model of what it looked like to "pray without ceasing" (1 Thess. 5:17, NKJV) and believe my prayers would make a difference.

DECIDING FOR CHANGE

After trying unsuccessfully to fix my marriage, I decided to follow Miss Clara's model. In the walk-in closet in our guest bedroom, I set up a prayer room like the one I saw in the movie. I brought the items I needed, including a chair, blanket, pen, and tape so I could write, journal, and hang scriptures all over the walls. In my own war room, I felt comfortable pouring out my heart and speaking aloud to the Holy Spirit. And that is exactly what I did. I looked up verses on forgiveness, searched out God's promises, and hung them on the walls. I surrounded myself with God's own words.

My mission was to do more than ask God for help. I spoke victory over my family and asked God to act on my behalf. I thanked Him daily for healing and restoration, even though I did not yet see any with my physical eyes. This went on for months, and it allowed me to develop the unexpected but powerful habit of aligning myself with the Holy Spirit. There, in my closet—my own war room—I learned the value of prayer and regular, consistent time talking to God and listening for His voice.

It's important to say that changing my husband was not my goal. I knew that only Brandon could make those choices. When I entered my prayer space, my goal was to find healing for myself. More and more, I longed for my moments with God in the morning. When my alarm went off each day, I'd grab a cup of coffee, settle into my little haven, connect with the Holy Spirit, and cry many tears. For thirty minutes each morning, I was fully engaged and 100 percent present with the Holy Spirit. I had a clear vision of what I wanted for my life and my marriage, and I spoke to God as if the vision was already in the making. I thanked Him for the leader my husband was becoming. I thanked Him for the healing of my heart. And I thanked him for the restoration of my trust. Amid the chaos, I took my eyes off the problem and thanked God for His solutions. By aligning myself with the Holy Spirit, inviting Him into my situation, and asking Him to move me forward, I gave Him control. This allowed Him to open up opportunities for change and healing.

Slowly but surely, I sensed that things were shifting. As I prayed, journaled, and meditated each morning, I felt the jagged pieces of my heart beginning to heal. Instead of being consumed with my husband's choices, responsibilities, and decisions, I concentrated on my own and focused on rediscovering what I wanted and what God had in store for me.

PRAYER IS THE ANSWER

As my healing progressed, my voice got stronger. This was a big change from where I had been in the deepest days of confusion when I lost myself and avoided saying or doing anything for fear of rocking the boat. Back then I had quit trusting my gut, but in my prayer room I once again became grounded and relearned how to listen to my heart and instincts. What a difference.

For example, after a rock-bottom moment, I realized there was nothing I could do to fix my marriage. Instead of trying to control the situation, I handed it entirely over to God. It was not exactly a mountaintop experience. In fact, it was the worst day of all. Brandon and I had argued, and even after my morning time in my prayer closet, I felt broken, defeated, and unsure of myself. Sitting in a Starbucks that I rarely visited, I listened to a conference call for work. With my eyes red from crying and my head hanging low, I sat with my earpiece, taking notes.

Out of nowhere, a gentleman walked up and said, "God wants you to know that it's all going to be OK!" That man had no idea how powerful his timing was. I obviously looked sad, but for him to offer me hope on my rock-bottom day, not hours after I'd just given it all to God—I was floored! Coincidence? I think not! The Holy Spirit was with me in my darkness. It wasn't the first time I experienced His comfort through the voice of another human being, and it wouldn't be the last.

A similar experience happened when my sister suggested I start working with someone like Jack Canfield or John Maxwell to further my personal development. I happened to get an email from Jack's team the next day, which led me to sign up for his Train the Trainer course. The course provided a wealth of personal development and growth opportunities for me and Brandon both. It truly answered my prayers for alignment and direction.

Another piece of the puzzle was even more surprising: during my meditation time one morning, I felt prompted to sign up for a bikini bodybuilding show. It was a first for me and seemed completely unrelated to anything else I was doing, yet it led to morning cardio sessions, during which I could listen uninterrupted to personal development audiobooks and podcasts. It also gave my husband mornings to himself to read and do his devotions. The Holy Spirit created the space we both needed for growth in a way that I never expected.

At the time, I didn't realize how important these happenings were. Looking back, I can see the domino effect they created and how it led to many breakthroughs in my marriage. All of it began with prioritizing genuine, faith-filled prayer and active listening, which allowed Him to move in mysterious and amazing ways.

Over time, our marriage continued to heal in little, often unnoticeable ways. As we spent more time seeking the direction of the Holy Spirit, each of us got closer to God. With our eyes fixed on

Him, our marriage prospered and our connection as a couple grew strong again. It wasn't an overnight process, but I know without a doubt that prayer was the catalyst.

Am I saying that prayer can fix all your problems? Yes, as a matter of fact, I am! You might not be in a place of personal crisis, as I was, but this truth still applies to whatever you're facing. Maybe you feel stuck in your job or career, or maybe you need to break old thought habits. Regardless of your need, prayer is the best way to close the gap between your current reality and the life you desire. As you pray consistently, your voice will become stronger, and you will see movement. This alignment with your Creator leads to alignment with yourself, which is a prerequisite for clarity, the next phase in the Dream Life Pathway and the topic of the next section of this book.

Before you move on, I want to remind you there is no deadline for your dreams. If you are ready to proceed, then by all means, complete the reflection below and then turn the page. However, if you feel like you're still in the thick of shifting your mind-set, reorienting your brain, and forging new neural pathways based on a lifestyle of gratitude, feel free to linger here. Reread this section. Do the exercises again. Pick up one of my gratitude journals, available at DeniseWalsh.com/books, and go through it for thirty days. Work on cultivating habits associated with these principles. It will pay off. You will never regret the time you invested in personal development. It is directly correlated with your success!

The Practice of Grateful, Intentional Prayer

INNER REFLECTION:

Prayer is talking to the Holy Spirit. Meditation is listening to what He has to say. In this exercise we will practice both.

1. What has been your struggle? A challenging relationship? A job you don't like? Health issues? Financial stress? A child (or children) who pushes your buttons? In what areas are you settling because you don't believe things will ever get any better? Are you settling because you are afraid to create more drama, because you just can't imagine things could ever be better, or because you are unsure of how to move forward—or all of the above? Or do you just need to learn how to slow down and break out of the sunup to sundown cycle of life-threatening busyness?

   Consider the above questions and write a brief but transparent response.

_____

_____

_____

_____

_____

_____

_____

_____

_____

_____

Next, spend two minutes of focused prayer simply talking with God, telling Him about your day and asking Him to be a part of it. You can also ask for clarity, guidance, and victory in the situations you wrote about above.

> 2. What impressions came to mind as you prayed?

_____

_____

_____

_____

In *War Room*, Miss Clara believed that the victory had already been won. Keep that in mind as you pray, and feel free to make the following prayers your own:

Thank You, Lord, for the all the blessings in my life. I am surrounded by family and friends who support, love, and encourage me to pursue my God-given passions. I am overflowing with love and ask that You use me to pour that love into others.

Today I choose love. Today I choose peace. Today I choose You. I trust that Your hands are in all situations and that all things will turn out for my good. I ask to see others and the world the way that You do, through eyes of compassion and love. May Your love overflow through me as You use my gifts and passions to bless the world. In Jesus's name, amen.

3. Now fill in the blanks below using some specifics from your story.

Thank You, God for:

_____

_____

_____

_____

_____

_____

Please move in the following situations in my life:

_____

_____

_____

_____

_____

_____

_____

_____

_____

4. List your three most pressing prayer requests below.

1 _____

_____

2 _____

_____

3 _____

_____

Now let's focus on the life that you want, not by offering a laundry list of problems to God but by asking the Holy Spirit to reveal what is best. Your job isn't to know *how* He will do it but to thank Him for moving, providing a path, and bringing clarity to a confusing situation. Take a moment to quiet your mind in order to listen to Him actively. Linger here in silence for at least five to ten minutes.

5. Write down what you believe the Holy Spirit is revealing about your situation and/or the prayers you lifted up to Him.

_____

_____

_____

_____

You may find, especially in the beginning, that it is hard to sustain extended periods of silent meditation. That's OK. The more you practice prayer and meditation, the easier it will be to wait on the Holy Spirit in expectancy.

> 6. End your prayer by saying, "Align me with Your will, and help me to see You in every aspect of my life."

As you cultivate a habit of quiet time with the Lord, let your heart begin to heal and allow God to move as He sees fit. Whatever form it takes or how long you spend in silence, remember that when you meditate on the things of God, you are changed.

PHASE #2

Pursue Clarity

Five

Your Joy Points to Your Passions

*If you can't figure out your purpose, figure
out your passion. For your passion will
lead you right into your purpose.*[30]

—Bishop T. D. Jakes

ACK IN CHAPTER 1, I talked about how *being* always precedes and takes precedence over *doing*. You cannot make or see positive, real change if you don't adjust your thoughts and mind-set first in order to bring yourself into alignment with the life you desire. But *being*, which begins in the mind, only leads to *doing*, which happens with your body, when you decide the specific direction you're moving in and articulate what actions will carry you there. That's why the second phase of the Dream Life Pathway is pursuing clarity. Clarity, which comes from within your heart and soul, will connect your head to your hands and feet, so to speak, so that you can take vital action to make your dreams reality.

This is the part of the process that people tend to find most intimidating, until they realize how natural it is. Clarity doesn't require an academic degree. You don't need to have grown up in the right social circles. It doesn't have an age minimum or maximum. Putting words to the dream that makes you tick only requires that you be *you*—no more and no less than you were created to be. Your unique passions, strengths, and interests, as well as your pet peeves and weaknesses, were curated by a wise Creator. He knit you together in your mother's body with purpose. Nothing about you is an accident. Nothing that has happened to you has the power to derail the destiny for which you were created. Romans 11:29 says, "God's gifts and his call are irrevocable." You were made for great things, and you already have everything you need to reach the calling He placed on your heart and the God-dreams He set within you.

If, in spite of that truth, you have found yourself stuck with lots of hope for the future and even more discouragement with where you are today, you're in the right place. By the time you finish this section, you'll be on fire with the fresh passion that comes from total clarity about your purpose. Plus, you'll have an actionable to-do list to move you closer to your dream life becoming reality. On the other hand, you already have a clear sense of that calling, congratulations! From here on, we will dive deeper into the mix of passions and strengths that make you, you so that you can form clear, actionable goals that will produce success.

LIFE-PRODUCING ACTION STARTS WITH LIFE-GIVING PASSION

When your passion and your purpose are aligned, reaching your dreams is effortless. Working toward your goals feels easy because you are in the zone. You have a fire in your belly, and one thing after another lines up along your path. The key, then, is to know exactly what your passion and purpose are.

This is important, especially because so many of us spend half our lives trying to find them. Even when we arrive at some understanding of our passion and purpose, few people are 100 percent sure that they've nailed it. For example, have you ever prayed, "OK, Holy Spirit, what else do You have for me? What's next for my life? What do You want me to do?" After praying, do you find yourself waiting for an unknown response or event to settle the issue, such as an external sign that points in a clear direction (typically the direction you already hoped for)? How long should you wait? Have you ever gone years without a clear next step? The waiting can seem endless. If this sounds familiar, you know how it feels to stay stuck.

That is where I was as a full-time clinical psychologist. I got into the field because I believed I could best serve the world there. I have a high level of belief in others and can often see who a person is becoming three steps ahead of when they see it themselves. I thought psychology was my way to pour that belief back into people and help them become all that God created them to be. Unfortunately, in the government mental health job that launched my psychology career, I discovered that the work day was more about policy, paperwork, and procedure than about people. Too often I felt like I was helping people who didn't really want help or who were wrapped up in a system that lacked the means to help them in the first place.

At twenty-six I went through what you might call a quarter-life crisis. All the work I did to obtain my master's degree and land my first job brought me to the disappointing conclusion that I didn't want to do this for the next thirty years of my life. Suddenly and unexpectedly, I was at a loss about what my next step was. I prayed with all my heart, "Holy Spirit, I don't want to stay in this career, but I don't know what else to do. Please tell me what You want for me."

Then I waited.

And waited.

And waited.

After a few job interviews I started doubting myself. I thought, "What if a new job turns out even worse and I find myself stuck all over again? Even if I dislike it, at least I know what to expect from my job in clinical psychology." I was terrified of making a wrong move, so I did nothing. I told myself I was waiting for the Holy Spirit to guide my next step clearly through an external or audible voice that would give me the courage to make a change. But really, I was looking outside for the answers He was already providing on the inside.

Looking back, I realize that another issue was hindering my progress. I couldn't move forward because my view of work in general was distorted by negativity. When I was in high school, every so often my mom would ask, "Why not get a job at the coffee shop?" I would confidently reply, "Because I love coffee shops, and I don't want to learn to hate them." In my mind, people hated their jobs and dreaded work. As far as I was concerned, that attitude was normal. What seemed abnormal was to love your job. Therefore, to preserve the things I loved and loved doing, I believed I had to separate them from my work. No wonder I had failed to pursue some of my passions and dreams! When I think about how many times the answer was right in front of me—or rather, right *within* me—I can't help but laugh or cry all over again!

Unfortunately, this is how most people operate. Instead of making important life decisions from a place of love, joy, peace, and fulfillment, they decide from places of fear, dread, and lack. How can they *not* feel powerless to make changes? With negative attitudes guiding their choices, mediocrity becomes the norm. The only possible outcome is to feel that they are spinning their wheels.

HAPPINESS STARTS ON THE INSIDE

Conventional wisdom holds that if our externals—everything from work to health to family and other observable realms—are all in order, our sense of success will manifest internally, and we will feel happy and content. However, research in positive psychology shows that the opposite is true: happiness fuels success, and not the other way around.

There are three ways to view your work situation: as a job, a career, or a calling.[31] Shawn Achor, author of *The Happiness Advantage*, writes that those with a job mentality tend to "see work as a chore and their paycheck as the reward."[32] Those who see their work as a career are more advancement-oriented, aware of growth opportunities, and invested in doing a good job. Those who view their work as a calling find their work fulfilling, not because of the external rewards but because it contributes to the greater good. For them, using their personal strengths gives them purpose and meaning. Not surprisingly, they "work harder and longer" because of it.[33]

During my stuck season of life, I thought the world's pie had already been divided up into fixed, unchangeable slices, which meant being stuck and unfulfilled was my lot. As I wrestled with the seeming adult reality that being in debt, hating my job, living like a zombie, and being conformist were normal, the dreams I had nurtured from childhood began shrinking. I could not see positive change coming anytime soon.

Was my misery truly rooted in reality? Was my current situation destined to be a life sentence? The answer is *no*. We have the power within us to do greater things! Jesus revealed the power of resurrection and the Holy Spirit when He exclaimed: "Very truly I tell you, whoever believes in me will do the works I have been doing, and they will *do even greater things than these*" (John 14:12, emphasis added). In spite of this truth, we often choose to sit back, stay quiet, and accept our current situations, as though we were helpless. We call our "stuckness" normal because it's what most people are experiencing, but this is the exact opposite of how Jesus has called us to live.

RECONNECTING WITH YOUR PASSIONS

Let's take a minute to get in touch with how you're feeling about your work and passions. Consider each question truthfully, and then record your thoughts.

1. Where are you in the range of work perceptions we discussed? Do you have a job, career, or calling?

2. Circle one: Are your <u>work</u> and <u>passions connected</u>, or have you <u>separated them</u>, like I did?

3. Circle one: Are you working within your God-given purpose? Yes   No

4. Circle one: Are you passionately pursuing your hobbies and interests? Yes   No

5. Circle one: Do you connect with anything that makes you feel passionate and joy-filled? Yes   No

6. If so, what?

Right now, I want you to decide that becoming aligned with your passion and purpose is something you want to do. Otherwise, why did you pick up this book? You want a life filled with joy, purpose, peace, and fulfillment, and you are willing to do the work necessary to attain it. The good news is, becoming unstuck is a decision, and you can make it—and start changing your life—right now.

When I decided that I was no longer comfortable accepting what I had tolerated as normal, I chose to believe the truth of Scripture, which showed me that I was called to be and do much more. It was the beginning of freedom, and change eventually took root. It started small, with identifying my passions and strengths. Then I applied that knowledge through consistent, daily choices to participate in endeavors connected to my passions.

I began embracing any and every opportunity that brought me joy. The decision-making process was not complicated: if the opportunity wasn't a total *yes* in my heart, then it was a 100 percent *no*.

Before long, because my passions were no longer separated from my work, my passions and work gradually melded.

Because of our passion for our faith, my husband and I joined a small group Bible study and became connected to a community of other Christ followers. In this small group we were introduced to the business that eventually transformed our lives. In 2007, we started our own network marketing business. I could not have anticipated it or envisioned it as the road God had for me. In fact, if He had revealed His plan from the beginning, it would have scared me silly. I was not business-savvy and had never done sales. I most certainly knew nothing about starting a business myself.

But that's what God does—"Immeasurably more than all we ask or imagine, according to his power that is at work within us" (Eph. 3:20). After I opened my heart to the Holy Spirit and committed myself to pursuing the passions He had set inside, He placed that business in front of me. It has allowed me to impact more people than I ever thought possible—people who want to improve their lives, this time through a system that can help them.

There are some points to note here. First, opportunities presented themselves because I said yes to them. And because I said yes, I had the courage to pursue them. That doesn't mean that I was fearless. When I began making changes, old thought patterns crept in, causing anxiety and worry. I started playing the comparison game and wondered whether I was cut out for this next step. Self-doubt and fear threatened my forward movement.

The human mind is wired to feel not good enough. Instead of seeing and valuing my own strengths, I focused on my weaknesses and the improvements I thought I needed. My eyes saw only my lack and my need to change. I found myself wondering whether I needed to be more like the people with whom I compared myself. I saw their strengths and wondered whether I needed to have the same ones. I wondered whether I needed to be more hip or professional, more bold and confident. Maybe I needed to be louder and own the room when I walked in. Or maybe I needed to take classes in sales or business.

When I complained to my husband about this one day, he said, "You have always been a good friend. Just do that."

"Really?" I thought. "Be a good friend? I *can* do that!"

The realization blew me away. I didn't need to fix my weaknesses or become more like the people I saw as successful. All I had to do was find what I loved and do what came naturally *to me*! Instead of trying to bolster skills that did not come as easily or bring me joy, I fed my existing strengths. When I did, they thrived. It was a game changer!

This process taught me that I already have the answers, the skill set, and the passion within me. Instead of looking outward, my challenge was to turn inward and connect with these assets and interests that were already part of me. I realized I had everything I needed to fulfill my God-designed purpose.

So do you. Your natural skills, abilities, and passions are within you for a reason. Do you know what they are?

By way of example, I have always been passionate about whole-person health and wellness. Helping people become the best possible version of themselves brings me indescribable joy. I also love connecting with friends over a good cup of coffee, reading books, and pushing myself to become better. Now, I've found a way to combine it all into my life's work. You could say it was there waiting for me the whole time. All I had to do was surrender to the possibility.

As the Bible teaches, "Take delight in the LORD, and he will give you your heart's desires. Commit everything you do to the LORD. Trust him, and he will help you" (Ps. 37:4–5, NLT). It is so freeing to realize that you lack nothing. Take this moment to declare to God and yourself that you will find and trust the natural inclinations, strengths, and passions that are already within you. It is a critical step on the path to lasting happiness.

INNER REFLECTION:

Your Joy-full Purpose

By his divine power, God has given us everything we need for living a godly life.

—2 Peter 1:3, NLT

Our natural interests and passions are meant to be pursued. God gives us all things, empowering us to live on purpose and for the greater good.

Living on purpose means that you are doing what you are good at and love to do, thereby accomplishing what is important to you (and God). When you live this way, the people, resources, and opportunities you need naturally gravitate toward you. Growth happens organically, and you live with a sense of peace and joy.

At the root of this lifestyle is trust. Proverbs 3:5–6 (NLT) reminds us of this: "Trust in the LORD with all your heart; do not depend on your own understanding. Seek his will in all you do, and he will show you which path to take." Trust empowers you to embrace the opportunities that present themselves when you are aligned with and pursuing your passions.

This is not a lack-focused mind-set. When you trust God, you realize that you don't need more and you don't need anything external. You know you already have everything you need. The only question is whether or not you are connected to it and actively using it.

1. What are your natural strengths? How would someone describe your personality? From the list below, circle the characteristics that come naturally to you.

- warm
- friendly
- generous
- adventurous
- timely
- hardworking
- fun
- introspective
- extroverted
- trustworthy
- respectful
- fair
- decisive
- authentic
- brave

- caring
- dependable
- giving
- sensitive
- understanding
- visionary
- detail-oriented
- creative
- strong
- _____
- _____
- _____
- _____
- _____
- _____

2. Circle the hobbies and interests to which you are naturally drawn:

- fitness
- nutrition
- hiking
- biking
- reading
- journaling/ writing
- running
- camping
- knitting
- hanging out with friends
- watching movies
- playing at the park
- karate
- scrapbooking

- photography
- painting/ drawing
- cooking
- dance
- crafting
- music
- gardening
- video games
- yoga
- swimming
- _____
- _____
- _____
- _____
- _____

Joy matters. It is an inner guidance system that confirms your alignment with purpose. I am not suggesting that anyone can or should be jumping for joy all the time; but the presence or absence of joy is a good indicator of whether you are on or off course. If joy and fulfillment are mainstays in your life, then your alignment is good. If joy and fulfillment are hard to come by, some course adjustments are probably in order.

    3. Consider the following questions and jot down the first things that come to mind.

    a) What brings you joy? What twenty things do you most love to do?

_____

_____

_____

_____

_____

_____

    b) What comes naturally or easily to you?

_____

_____

_____

_____

    c) Fill in the blank: Time flies when I'm:

_____.

4. Do your answers on these questions reveal any common themes? If so, what are they?

_____

_____

_____

_____

5. What interests, hobbies, or passions will you make a commitment to pursuing now that you have identified them? How will you pursue them?

_____

_____

_____

_____

Six

YOUR PASSIONS POINT TO YOUR PURPOSE

*We all have two choices: We can make
a living or we can design a life.*[34]

—JIM ROHN

I HOPE BY NOW you're starting to get excited about what's happening in your life. As you identify and connect with your joys, interests, and strengths, you should feel passion building up. When your vision is clear, it ignites a fire in your belly. That fire launches you out of bed each morning and propels you to act in favor of your dreams. That is a powerful way to live, and it is only possible with a vision in mind.

The truth is that most people don't know what they want. They lack a clear vision and don't know what they want their lives to look like. Without a specific dream to move toward, they get stuck in places they don't want to be. They're miserable and unsure of which changes will dig them out. This is no fault of their own. After all, how can you follow a road map that has no destination?

If your destination is still unclear, don't despair. This chapter will help you leave your visionless state behind.

GET YOUR EYES OFF THE GRASS

There are two things you need to know at this point, now that you've started to identify what brings you joy and gain a sense of your calling. Both are tied to happiness and how it intersects with your unique purpose.

This isn't an escape act.

The first is this: designing your dream life is more than an elaborate escape act from the life and circumstances you are living today. If your dream is nothing more than a well-articulated description of the grass on the other side of your fence, it will bring you neither true happiness nor success. The happiness that comes with achieving and living your best life is rooted in the deeper sense of joy that comes from living in alignment with yourself, your Creator, and the purpose for which you were designed. Getting away from your circumstances is not enough. You've got to dream bigger than that. Instead of merely escaping, you must move toward the thing that ignites that fire in your belly, the thing that will keep you dreaming even as you reach new levels of success.

Purpose and dream go hand-in-hand. If your dream lacks purpose, it will not satisfy you in the long term. It will be little more than a vacation; before long, you'll return to business and life as usual, and you'll find yourself longing for more. But when you build your dream with purpose in mind, not only will you succeed, but the benefits and happiness will be lasting. It will carry you on to bigger, better things and new, higher levels of achievement. There is no limit to what you will be able to accomplish when you marry your dreams with your calling.

It isn't all about you.

That brings me to the second thing you need to know: your dream cannot be all about what you'll get out of it. It is OK to want your dream life to make your daily life easier and more fun. It is OK for your dream to take into account material possessions you'd like to have. There's nothing inherently wrong with those desires, and you shouldn't feel guilty about them. Your dream life should make it possible for you to enjoy luxuries that are out of your reach now. But whether you want the freedom to travel without debt, more time with the people you love, help around your house, a Mercedes, seventeen designer bags, or just to get the bill collectors off your back, your dream has to be bigger than you, because your purpose is greater than you. Your purpose is about more than your happiness.

Your dream life will start out making your life better, but it has to end with improving others' as well, or it will never be enough. Most likely, it won't even be enough to keep you motivated to chase your goals when the going gets tough. If you haven't already noticed, the work required to build your best life from the ground up requires a lot of change, and change is downright uncomfortable. That is why most people opt to stay where they are, even if they hate being there. Getting uncomfortable and trying something different can seem like a bridge too far, even if the bridge leads to their dreams.

A dream without purpose may spark your interest for a while, but it won't ignite a fire in your bones. It will never bring you real, transformative joy. That is only found in pursuing a dream that is aligned with the specific set of gifts, talents, and passions that God gave you so that you could change the world, or at least your little slice of it. You were made to make an impact. You've probably already changed some lives up to this point! But when you achieve your dream and start living out the God-given purpose in your life, your impact and happiness will be explosive. Your life and your community will never be the same.

Life Purpose Statement

INNER REFLECTION:

Reconnecting with who you are and what you love means becoming consciously aware of your purpose. You are now ready to ignite that awareness by creating a life purpose statement. Your life purpose statement has two functions: it will declare your mission and serve as a guide for your daily decisions. However attractive a choice might appear to be, it is counterproductive unless it lines up with you and your purpose. If a past choice is out of kilter with where you're headed, now is the time to move away from it. Because it is an indispensable tool to help you navigate around obstacles and ensure you're taking the most direct route toward your best life, you'll want to keep it close to you at all times.

Writing your life purpose statement is not hard. Use the following exercises to help you develop yours.

1. List two personal qualities about yourself that you are the most proud of (e.g., my love for and high belief in others, work ethic, loyalty, etc.).

_____

_____

2. List one or two ways in which you enjoy expressing these qualities to benefit others (e.g., "I like to encourage other

people to go after their goals," "I like to see projects finished and with excellence," "I take pride in knowing that my loved ones know that our relationship isn't conditional").

_____

_____

3. Now shift your focus beyond yourself and assume for a moment that you are living in a perfect world. In this ideal scenario, I want you to pay attention to what is "fixed" about the world. What problem is missing or adjusted or perfected such that the world is exactly as it should be for everyone? (For example, when I look around the real world, it grieves my soul to see people living beneath their full potential and struggling to grasp just how incredible they are. In my perfect world, everyone knows and focuses on their amazing, God-given strengths and lives out their full calling.)

_____

_____

_____

_____

_____

_____

4. How do your strengths and the way you use them for others fix the problem you identified in question 3? (In my example, my love for others and belief in them is expressed as encouragement to pursue their dreams and goals. By doing this, they will understand what they are truly capable of and be able to pursue and attain their highest purpose.)

_____

_____

_____

_____

5. Combine your answers to questions 1 through 4 into a single statement, written in the present tense, that describes your place in a perfect world, as you envisioned it. (Example: My purpose is to use my love and belief in others to encourage them to go after their goals. In this way, I will be able to create a world where everyone is full of joy, has high self-confidence, and knows just how awesome they really are.)

My purpose is to:

_____

_____

_____

_____

_____

_____

Once you have written out your life purpose statement, make it the focal point of your thoughts and decisions. Over time, and with intentional effort, you will become the person it describes and will make the world better in the process. This is how you will be able to achieve the real change, and real happiness, you desire.

6. Write down your life purpose statement somewhere you can see it often, or better yet, make it the background on your phone. Read it when you get up in the morning and before you go to bed at night. Allow the vision to move from your head to your heart.

Seven

A CLEAR PURPOSE MAKES WAY FOR SUCCESS

The first principle of success is desire—knowing what
you want. Desire is the planting of your seed.

—ROBERT COLLIER

O K, FRIEND. YOU'VE done the all inner work it took to get here. You took back control of your mind and shifted the narrative from fear and negativity to hope and destiny. You've developed a habit of prayer and meditation. You looked inward and (re)discovered your passions and source of joy. You aligned yourself with your purpose and articulated your very own mission statement. You have done some serious work. Now it's time to play. In this chapter and the next, you are going to let your imagination run wild. This is where you get to dream your way into your desired future!

WHAT YOU REALLY, REALLY WANT

A couple of years ago I invited my team to a Come as You Will Be Party. Yes, you read that correctly: Come as You *Will Be*. It was an epic event at a hilltop venue with a gorgeous view. The theme of was from Proverbs 29:18 (KJV): "Where there is no vision, the people perish." Each place setting included a pair of binoculars—fitting for a tree house party about gaining new perspective for the future, don't you think?—inscribed with the verse.

In keeping with the theme, I challenged guests to show up as the people they envisioned themselves being in ten years' time. They would dress and speak like—they would *be*—themselves in the year 2025, living their dreams out as if they had achieved them. To do this, they needed clarity about whom and how they wanted to be, what they wanted to have, and all they wanted to experience in the coming ten years. That meant giving serious thought to their dreams ahead of the party.

Greeted by signs that said "Welcome to 2025," guests arrived in costumes depicting their individual visions. Some dressed in beachwear and described themselves as the retired owners of a beachside bed-and-breakfast. Others arrived with several babies tied to their hips to signify their vision of having more children. Some posted pictures of their dream homes on their phones and talked about moving day. One attendee described his experience at the Hollywood premiere of a movie that was based on a book he wrote.

I arrived in a blue dress with my hair and makeup professionally done. I spoke about my first TED Talk and explained that by the time I flew home from the event, the video of my speech had already gone viral. I carried a business card that listed some of my accomplishments:

- Triple Black Diamond leader[*]

- International speaker, trainer, and *New York Times* best-selling author

- As seen on her TED Talk, *American Ninja Warrior*, and Oprah's Favorite Things

- World-renowned basketball mom, loving wife, and devoted philanthropist

---

[*] This hypothetical rank in the company would come with a $300,000 per month paycheck and the prestige of being the very top income earner.

The event was memorable, but preparing for it required real work. Many of my teammates seemed a tinge resentful about that. It stretched them hard, and it got uncomfortable. But here's the thing: if you are waiting for your dream to fall from the sky into your lap, you will be waiting a long time. What's more, developing a strong, clear personal vision doesn't happen in a vacuum. It happens amid the ups and downs of real life. It will require a lot of you, sometimes when you feel you don't have a lot to give. But it's always worth it, and once you get past the hard part, it's so much fun.

Those who took on the challenge I gave them for that event successfully created new visions for themselves and their families and devised plans to achieve what they envisioned. The process was rigorous, but it changed them, and not just in the short term. Thinking about what you want to achieve and who you want to be will change you too.

Even more than that, it will also change those around you. The journey of deciding exactly what you want impacts everyone in your sphere of influence, not only because of your end goal but because of who you become in the process. Your actions, your dreams, are already changing lives. Yours is just the starting point.

What Do I Want?

INNER REFLECTION:

Gratitude, prayer, and meditation on God's Word help us achieve clarity for the road ahead. Approach the following exercises with that in mind, and you will make great strides.

1. Your dream is not one-dimensional, because life is multifaceted. To flesh out the details of your dream, fill in the following lists with between twenty and thirty items each (the more the better).

THINGS I WANT TO DO

_____

_____

_____

_____

_____

_____

_____

_____

_____

_____

_____

_____

_____

_____

_____

_____

_____

_____

_____

_____

_____

_____

_____

_____

_____

_____

_____

THINGS I WANT TO BE

_____

_____

_____

_____

_____

_____

_____

_____

_____

_____

_____

_____

_____

_____

_____

_____

_____

_____

_____

_____

_____

_____

_____

_____

_____

_____

_____

_____

_____

_____

_____

_____

_____

THINGS I WANT TO HAVE

_____

_____

_____

_____

_____

_____

_____

_____

_____

_____

_____

_____

_____

_____

_____

_____

_____

_____

_____

_____

_____

_____

_____

_____

_____

2. Alone or with a partner, such as your spouse, answer the question, "What do I want?" Say whatever comes to mind—ideas, experiences you want to have, trips you'd like to take, etc. The nature of your answers might change as you go along. You might start out saying, "I want to be happy," and end up realizing that you long for certain relationships to be healed. You might become aware of experiences you want to have. You might even arrive at a definition of what being happy means for you. Nothing is off limits.

In question 1, you wrote your responses, but the goal here is to speak your answer to the question "What do I want?" out loud, allowing honest answers to bubble up from within. While you talk, have your partner record your answers here. Or, if you're doing this alone, record yourself as you speak and then take notes here as you listen back to the recording. (You may find you need extra paper. That's OK.)

_____

_____

_____

_____

_____

_____

_____

_____

_____

_____

_____

_____

_____

_____

_____

_____

_____

_____

_____

_____

_____

_____

_____

_____

_____

_____

_____

_____

_____

_____

_____

_____

_____

_____

_____

_____

3. Now I want you to imagine your life as if all those things you want to be, have, and do have come to pass. Write a letter to yourself, and date it five years from today. In your letter, talk about all the things five-years-from-now you have accomplished and earned. Talk about who you are, how you are, and what experiences have shaped you. Take into account everything you wrote and spoke about in questions 1 and 2. Write your letter in the past tense, as if you have already completed it all.

_____

_____

_____

_____

_____

_____

_____

_____

_____

_____

_____

_____

_____

_____

_____

_____

_____

_____

Congratulations! You just set your internal GPS. You've given your mind, heart, and body a sense of what to work toward. You're well on your way to a life of success and significance.

Eight

PLAN YOUR DREAM DAY

Your time is limited, so don't waste
it living someone else's life.

—STEVE JOBS

WHEN I ORGANIZED the Come as You Will Be Party, Brandon and I were working our way through the most challenging period in our marriage. At the time, we were not on the same page about where our lives were headed. I thought, "What a time to ask my husband to dream about our future!"

Tough as it was, I asked him anyway. First, however, I took his feelings into account. I knew I needed to create the space—a slice of heaven, so to speak—for Brandon to hear the Holy Spirit, connect with himself, and connect with me. I thought being in nature and away from computers, TVs, and interrupting children would give us the chance to talk and dream together. So, I reserved a boat for us to go fishing at a nearby lake.

It was a calm, overcast day, and Brandon and I were alone on the water. On the boat ride, I played an audiobook on speakerphone for us to listen to. The fish weren't biting, but the atmosphere was perfect.

Just like my team, Brandon was a bit grouchy at first that I was asking him to drill down into the specifics of what he wanted for himself and for us and out of life in general. But once he allowed his mind to run free, he became excited about the dreams he started to verbalize. For about thirty minutes, I asked him, "What do you want?" and wrote down his answers for him. Any time he stopped, I repeated the question: "What do you want?" I did this without judging or trying to reason out what he said. My job was to listen and accurately capture his responses.

Afterward, Brandon did the same for me, and by the time we were finished, we were both excited! We talked about what we wanted and how we could accomplish it without compromising or skimping on our visions. The experience helped me to become better aligned with my husband and understand where he was coming from. The same was true for him. In fact, the experience proved to be a turning point in our healing journey.

Because the outing was so productive, we took it several steps further. Each of us envisioned and wrote in detail about our version of an ideal day, our dream day. When I say detail, I mean detail. We asked, "What do I do on my dream day? How do I feel? Where do I live? How do my relationships look and feel?" Answering these questions at length brought clarity to my vision of an ideal day and sharpened my vision for life.

Below is what I wrote. Obviously, it's entirely personal, and your particulars will be different. The idea is to express yourself fully, whatever your fine points might be. I encourage you to read mine, not so I can tout my dreams but because I believe the example will inspire you to dream more freely.

MY DREAM DAY

I awaken just before sunrise and begin my day with an intense workout. I feel healthy, invigorated, and fit. Starting my day with a run, a kickboxing class, or weight training clears my mind and gives me necessary space to think. I use this time to continue my learning and listen to personal development materials.

I arrive home before my children awaken and start my miracle morning in my war room. I feel such connection, alignment, and peace after I read, pray, and align my heart with the Holy Spirit. Brandon is doing his reading in his space, and we are able to connect before the day's routines begin. During breakfast, we sit together and chat about the books we are reading and about upcoming family adventures. We also discuss our personal and combined goals. We are both committed to lifelong learning and growth, and we love doing both together. We sit in our reading nook and look outside at the woods that surround our home. We feel such peace in this serene setting.

After a family breakfast that is full of laughter and goofy fun with our children, one of us drops them off at school, and we both head to work. We love that we have several different businesses that offer residual income and the time to chase our dreams and goals. I love creating content and have my heart set on adding value to people in order to push them outside their comfort zones and into who they were created to be. I feel fulfilled and joy filled as I do my work. I'm thankful to strike a balance between creating content and working with people in my webinars, workshops, and live events.

It's exciting and humbling to know that our team is thriving all over the world, and I am a frontrunner in bringing the company's message of friendship, fun, and freedom to people everywhere. I'm encouraged knowing that people want to be part of something bigger than themselves, and our team is a place for them to be inspired, reconnected with their purpose, and healthier every step of the way. I cannot help but give thanks for the freedom of time, the flexibility to travel, and the ability to meet amazing people all over the world. I am aware that I am in love with the life I have created for myself.

On my dream day, I give thanks for the help with which we are blessed. Our housekeeper, who comes three times a week to help with laundry, housework, and general indoor maintenance, is amazing. Our handyman ensures that the pool and home repairs are up to date. They both offer so much value and love to our family. Our lives would not be the same without them.

My personal trainer/nutritionist helps me plan meals and holds me accountable to my health goals. My personal shopper brings fresh vegetables and other groceries every other day, making it easy for me to cook healthy meals that our family enjoys. Learning to cook with simple, fresh ingredients has made dinnertime fun for all of us. The boys love to help, and they enjoy their vegetables because they are a part of God's creation. I am happy and grateful to have such support in my life.

I pick up my kiddos after school and am a fully engaged mom for the rest of the day. I drive them to sports, help them with their homework, and make dinner for them. My children know that I am 100 percent present with them. They know I love my work, but they know I love them even more.

When Brandon comes home, we enjoy a family meal, talking and laughing about our day. After our kids go to bed, Brandon and I have time to connect before he heads to bed and I head to the computer to work with my clients and team members for a few hours.

Our lives are filled with joy, gratefulness, and love as we impact each other and influence the world. We travel together once each quarter, always in first class with direct flights to our destinations. We travel internationally at least once a year as a family, although I go more often for speaking engagements. Our favorite vacation spot is our two-thousand-square-foot condo in Sarasota, Florida. We often bring family and members of our team to enjoy the condo with us.

I am thrilled to be a *New York Times* best-selling author and transformational leader who provides experiential learning and growth experiences to those who want to evolve into their best selves. It is so much fun to receive daily emails about how my TED Talk and *Dream Cast* podcast are making a difference for others.

I am thriving in all areas of my life, including my health, relationships, and career. I am consistently in alignment with who I am created to be, and my dreams come easily and effortlessly, even more than I ever imagined possible.

Notice how clear and detailed my description is. Note too that in addition to describing events and actions, I shared my feelings and outlook while involving all my senses and emotions.

I cannot stress the value of this enough. It is *so* powerful, and I have found it helpful to revisit the exercise regularly, since my version of an ideal day evolves as my family changes and my children grow. It is also a great way to encourage yourself and get excited all over again about the big dreams you're chasing.

The Best Day of Your Life

INNER REFLECTION:

Find your little slice of heaven and settle in. In chapter 4, we talked about my personal war room, where I am free to reconnect and pray. Your space could be anywhere. If not in nature or a prayer closet, then maybe it's poolside with your journal and a book, in a spa with a glass of wine, on the golf course, or even in the shower. Wherever your eyes and heart are most open to hearing the Holy Spirit and communing with Him, make time there to think about exactly what your dream day looks like. Use the following questions to help you envision the details.

This is a powerful exercise, so don't rush it. I give you permission to dream *passionately* for as long as it takes to express everything on your heart.

1. What do you do when you get up in the morning? Who is there with you? How do you feel as you go through this part of your day?

_____

_____

_____

_____

_____

_____

2. What does your environment look like? What features does your space include? A pool? Hot tub? How does being in this place make you feel?

_____

_____

_____

_____

3. Are you dressing up to commute to work or working at home, perhaps in your pajamas? What emotions are you aware of as you get ready for the day?

_____

_____

_____

_____

4. If you commute, how do you get to work? Do you have a driver? A private plane? A pilot on standby?

_____

_____

_____

5. Do you take vacations and/or have a vacation home? Describe them/it and who is with you. What emotions are associated with taking these trips?

_____

_____

_____

_____

6. In short, if you could do anything and be anyone (and money and resources were *not* an issue) what would you do? Who would you be? How would you feel?

_____

_____

_____

_____

7. Incorporate the above answers and others that come to mind into a detailed description of your dream day.

_____

_____

_____

_____

_____

_____

_____

_____

_____

_____

_____

_____

_____

_____

_____

_____

_____

_____

_____

_____

_____

8. Imagine what your life would be like if your joy, peace, fulfilment, and gratitude were increased by a factor of ten. Describe it in your own words.

_____

_____

_____

_____

9. On a scale of one to ten (with ten being most amazing), describe your level of peace and joy as you experience your dream day.

1 2 3 4 5 6 7 8 9 10

Next, let's move from planning your dream day to imagining your dream life. I want you to consider your dream life from seven different perspectives: family, friendships, finances, health, hobbies, business, and giving back. You'll describe the details of your future in each of the following areas, just as you did with your dream day. (I've included my examples to help you brainstorm.) We will revisit this seven-point list later, so establishing a clear vision for each point now is important.

As you write, allow yourself to get excited about what each area of your life ideally looks like. For Brandon and me, the clarity this exercise gave us about what we wanted our lives to look like got us so excited that we couldn't help but move toward what we pictured. Don't move on from this chapter until you feel the same way!

Family

Example: Brandon and I have a healthy marriage and a strong friendship. We communicate daily, are working toward similar goals, and have deep trust in one another. Our relationship is rich and full of life. We go on couples' weekends once or twice a year and enjoy a minimum of two date nights per month.

My relationship with my sons is full of laughter. I take each of them out once a month for date nights, and we create amazing memories.

Our family and extended family get together for most holidays, and we always have a good time.

_____

_____

_____

_____

_____

_____

_____

_____

Friendships

Example: I am so grateful for my friendships with women who truly know me and love me. They challenge me to live my best life because they are living their best life. I feel challenged when we are together, yet deeply supported. I am so grateful for our weekend getaways, retreats, work relationships, and the life we get to lead together.

_____

_____

_____

_____

_____

_____

_____

_____

_____

_____

_____

_____

Finances

Example: I am earning $3 million per year. I have several streams of income and am able to travel, enjoy life, and save for our future. I give 10 percent of my income each month to charities or causes of our choosing. I am saving 10 percent for good measure and putting away 10 percent each month for the children.

I am able to spend money freely and give freely as income steadily flows into our home.

_____

_____

_____

_____

_____

_____

_____

_____

_____

_____

_____

Health

Example: I am a clean eater who lives life on plan. I maintain a fit 127- to 133-pound body weight, and I feel strong and healthy. I am always stage ready, meaning I'm happy with the way my body looks and confident while speaking on stage.

I do more bodybuilding shows to push myself to the limit and beyond. I find new physical activities that challenge me and help me stay in shape the way bodybuilding always has. As a result of my fit lifestyle, my family and extended family have begun taking excellent care of their bodies so that we can enjoy a long and happy life together.

_____

_____

_____

_____

_____

_____

_____

_____

_____

Hobbies

Example: Along with reading, writing, and outdoor activities, I learn and grow daily by expanding my network, asking questions, and leveling up my dreams. I learn new skills that help me to be an even better leader, a stronger businesswoman, and a more effective coach who can help anyone achieve their dreams.

My family goes on two international vacations a year, and we are able to show our boys the world! My sons learn so much on our travels and look forward to this family time. We have visited every continent, and as a family activity we learn a little bit of the language before visiting a new country. Traveling inspires us with a bigger view of the world. We often connect with fellow travelers, and some become our lifelong friends!

_____

_____

_____

_____

_____

_____

_____

_____

Business

Example: I work six hours a day and feel ful-filled. I am impacting those around me through speaking, workshops, webinar series, and coaching events. I am watching my team grow and flourish as I help them to penetrate their perceived ceilings. Pouring into people, seeing them three steps ahead of where they see themselves, and spreading joy are my joys. I call out the good in others and breathe life into people. When they are around me, they know they are loved and cared for. God works through me to spread His love.

_____

_____

_____

_____

_____

_____

_____

_____

_____

_____

_____

Giving back

Example: In honor of my grandmother, who paid for all of my college education, I have created a scholarship fund for Grand Valley State University, my undergraduate school.

Because of my love for running trails, I donate funds to a trail in my community and have named it DEW Running Trail (my initials are DEW).

I love to give back locally and globally, and I teach my children the gift of service by going on international mission trips and volunteering at local food pantries.

I have a plan in place to leave a legacy for my children. They will have the brain space to dream and fulfill their God-given purposes because of our hard work and blessings.

_____

_____

_____

_____

_____

_____

Now that you know what you want, it's time to go get it!

PHASE #3

Take Consistent, Empowered Action

Nine

TURN YOUR DREAMS INTO PLANS

*Our goals can only be reached through a vehicle of a plan,
in which we must fervently believe, and upon which we
must vigorously act. There is no other route to success.*

—PABLO PICASSO

ISN'T DREAMING FUN? Now that you are clear about what you want in life, you are ready to make it real. How? By converting your dreams into specific, measurable goals and objectives. Dreaming is a vital step toward the fulfilled life, but dreams alone cannot get you where you want to be. You need to build goals in support of your dreams, and you need to put deadlines in place to ensure your forward motion.

Sounds like common sense, right? So why don't most people do it? I think the truth is that most of us were never taught how. Think back to your schooling and family life. Did you have a life-skills class that taught you good success habits? Did you and your loved ones talk about goal-setting over dinner? Did you grow up around persistent dreamers who set goals and achieved them? This sure wasn't my story. Because most of us never learned these skills, we play without a game plan and succumb to the pitfalls of fear, bitterness, self-sabotage, and settling for less. We don't take the right action to pursue our dreams; therefore, we are easy prey to the paralyzing fears of rejection, of failure, and even of our own success. Without a good offense to keep us on track, we quit almost before we get started. High achievers typically fare better because they actively set goals and deadlines to support their dreams, and numerous studies bear out the strong link between goal-setting and task performance.[35] But statistically, the setting and keeping of goals seems *not* to be the habit of the majority.

You can train yourself to make it your way of life. If you will commit to the exercises in the pages and chapters ahead, you will learn how to frame—and stick to—meaningful goals and support them with action steps that lead to success.

GETTING DOWN TO BUSINESS

To begin, I want you to revisit the seven life categories you considered when you were imagining your dream day: family, friendships, finances, health, hobbies, business, and giving back. Choose the one that stands out most. It might be the one that creates the most excitement for you or one that has the greatest impact on other areas of your life. For example, a goal of losing fifty pounds might impact your confidence, family relationships, ability to engage in certain activities, and even your energy levels. Setting a goal to rekindle a drifting marriage would impact the rest of your family, not to mention your overall happiness, performance at work, and even your health. Or your dream might be more business-minded. You might set a goal to become a *New York Times* best-selling author who also gives podcast and TV interviews. Or you might set your sights on reaching the top level of your company.

Whatever your goals, they come in two basic types: *results goals* and *process goals*. Results goals, which are also called target goals, focus on the end result you want to achieve. Process goals focus on what you will do to get there.

Let's run this out using an example from my own experience. After my second son was born, I struggled to shed the last extra ten to fifteen pounds of baby weight. For three years I carried around thoughts that said, "Moms always have some belly fat," and, "I don't have time or energy to change my diet." Finally I decided I wanted to make a healthy change.

I have always been athletic and loved to exercise, but with two young children, working out for several hours each day was no longer feasible. I quickly realized I wouldn't be able to resort to the plans and solutions that had made weight loss easier for me in earlier stages of my life. Still, despite my excuses, I knew that I wanted to improve my health, so I decided to tackle it like I would any other plan: by turning my dream of being trim again into a goal.

I started by writing my target goal in my journal:

I weigh a healthy and fit 130 pounds by May 2016.

Then I wrote out the *process goal*, also known as a daily practice goal, that would support my target goal. Process goals map out the logistics of how you will reach your target, as follows:

I will exercise a minimum of one hour per day six days a week. I will follow a clearly designed meal plan from Monday through Saturday and will have one off-plan day on Sunday.

In order to balance your long-term vision with your daily practices, you'll need to have both target and process goals. I also recommend focusing on one goal and one result at a time. Dividing your attentions, especially when you are still learning this process, can be challenging. Choosing one target goal at a time will help you stay focused, see achievement, and cross goals off your to-do list.

When you're writing your goals, wording matters. Always express goals in the present tense, as if they are already happening. The acronym *SMARTER* is often used to communicate other helpful guidelines for goal-setting. Goals should be:

- Specific

- Measurable and motivating

- Achievable

- Realistic

- Time-bound

- Evaluated

- Reviewed[36]

With this acronym in mind, let's examine my target goal: "I weigh a healthy and fit 130 pounds by May 2016." The stated goal is:

- *Specific.* It establishes a clear outcome (a specific weight).

- *Measurable.* The goal states a specific weight that will be reached. It is also *motivating,* because being fit and healthy are the end results envisioned by the goal-setter.

- *Achievable.* Based on my starting weight and the time period allowed for weight loss, the goal is reasonable.

- *Realistic.* Not only should your goal be possible, but you must *believe* it is possible.

- *Time-bound.* The goal has a clear endpoint.

- *Evaluated.* The goal-setter continually assesses the goal and his or her progress.

- *Reviewed.* The goal-setter tweaks his or her approach and attitude in order to maintain focus and ensure progress.

All of these factors contribute to the goal-setter's success. For me, the fact that the goal was motivating meant I had a picture in mind of how I would feel when my goal is reached. This helped me to say no to s'mores and yes to the treadmill. The measurable nature of the goal ensured that my success was not subjective. On May 31, 2016, anyone could put me on a scale and tell whether or not I had succeeded. Talk about accountability!

Because my goal was clear, I was able to outline the exact action steps it would take to succeed. I followed the plan, pursued my process goals, and met my results goal. I even ended up entering and participating in a bikini bodybuilding competition in the process! I'm telling you, goal-setting is a game-changer for your dreams.

What dreams will you turn into specific, clearly defined goals? Some of them are staring you in the face. Now is the time to look them dead in the eye.

Choosing Your Target

INNER REFLECTION:

Goals are not set in a vacuum, and no goal stands alone. Goal-setting touches on the interconnectedness of your dreams and passions. Yet your plan of attack must start somewhere, so let's use the following exercises to choose a starting point.

1. Which of the seven areas of life (i.e., family, friendships, finances, health, hobbies, business, and giving back) would you like to work on first?

_____

2. Why is this area the best starting place?

_____

_____

_____

_____

3. How will improvements in this area positively impact other areas of your life?

_____

_____

4. Next, you will turn your dreams for this area into tangible, realistic, and exciting goals. Start by writing your desires in the left column. (For now, let's focus just on your dreams in the one area you plan to start with.) Then on the right, write a goal for reaching that dream. Remember to use the acronym SMARTER, write in the present tense, and be positive. You're welcome to use the following examples as templates.

DREAMS AND DESIRES	CLEAR, SPECIFIC, TIME-FOCUSED GOALS
I want to own a beautiful home someday.	By May of 2020, I own a two-thousand-square-foot condo in Bradenton, Florida.
I want to vacation with my family.	In May of 2018 I am taking my family on a Disney cruise.
I want to write a book to help others.	My book will be published no later than December 2019.
I want to lose weight.	By October 2019, I will have lost twenty pounds.

DREAMS AND DESIRES	CLEAR, SPECIFIC, TIME-FOCUSED GOALS

5. Goal fulfillment in the area of your life that most impacts the others can initiate a quantum leap forward, so let's start there. Pick the dream and goal from above that you want to work on first. We will call this your Dream Life goal, because it will have a cascading effect that will change everything. It will launch you into brand-new territory.

   Rewrite it below, and under it write how you're going to make it happen. (These are your process, or daily practice, goals.)

   My Dream Life goal is:

   _____

   _____

   (Example: By October 2019, I will have lost twenty pounds and will be working out five days a week.)

DAILY PRACTICE/PROCESS GOALS

_____

_____

_____

_____

(Examples: I will work out five days a week. I will find a nutrition plan that supports my weight-loss goals, and I will follow it with only one cheat meal per week.)

Now pick one or two of these process goals to work on right now. Once you master these and turn these practices into habits, you can move on to the other daily goals that support your big Dream Life goal.

6. What emotions are stirred up as you write about your goal?

_____

_____

7. Which emotions point to roadblocks in your thinking?

_____

_____

8. What has prevented you from committing to and/or fulfilling this goal in the past?

_____

_____

_____

_____

Let's be real. Setting a Dream Life goal can be nerve-racking! The very thought of making a commitment can stir up all sorts of limiting beliefs about yourself, your role in the world, and what you are able to accomplish. Do not be intimidated by the onslaught. We will talk in more detail later in this book about how to address pitfalls and dream-killers, but for now simply acknowledge your negating thoughts and replace them with the truth. Your goals are now free to succeed!

Ten

The Power of Believing Your Own Words

*Truly I tell you, if anyone says to this mountain,
"Go, throw yourself into the sea," and does not
doubt in their heart but believes that what they
say will happen, it will be done for them.*

—Mark 11:23

BRANDON AND I were at our Come as You Will Be Party when our CEO sent us a text to say that we had hit our target for month five of a big, six-month goal we were working toward. In order to be promoted to Black Diamond, we had to earn a certain income for six months in a row. Making it to the fifth month was an important milestone for us.

We had been working on the Black Diamond goal for several years, and we had failed more than once. Twice, we had made it to the four-month mark, only to miss the magic number in month five. The first time we hit our month-four target, I thought we had the promotion in the bag. When it fell through, I was devastated. I felt like we had worked so hard and failed anyway. There was a sense of defeat and, I admit, anger that I directed at myself for not achieving the goal. I thought in an almost spiteful way, "If it's going to happen, it will happen."

My words transferred responsibility and, therefore, my power to succeed to someone other than myself. I said I wanted to achieve Black Diamond rank, but my belief and effort didn't line up. Missing the promotion had left me jaded. Somewhere deep down I tried to shield myself from another failure. I would say out loud, "I'm going Black Diamond!" but the voice of doubt shouted in the back of my mind, "Yeah, right. You didn't make it last time, so what makes you think you'll do it this time?"

My doubt was profound. It permeated my thoughts and affected my behavior in insidious ways. Because part of me didn't think we'd reach Black Diamond anyway, I quit really trying. I self-sabotaged by going through the motions, giving up emotionally, and withholding my full effort. Not surprisingly, we missed the promotion a second time.

Two years after we missed Black Diamond the first time, I decided that our goal wasn't going to happen on its own, and if I wanted a different outcome than the one we'd already experienced twice, I would have to do something different. What I'm about to teach you about the power of affirmation is the very something different that propelled our business all the way to our seemingly impossible goal—and beyond.

SPEAK LIFE

For a while now, since you started this book, you've been talking about your dreams, thinking about them, writing them down, and talking and thinking some more. I hope you are feeling excited, confident, and motivated. But I want you to know that if you are still hearing a voice in the back of your head that says, "It won't happen," it doesn't mean you're not doing this right. It is possible to be solidly in the sweet spot of the Dream Life Pathway and still notice doubts trying to creep in at the corners of your mind.

As we talked about in the first section, where we laid the foundation for your dream life by examining your mind-set, the key is this: having negative thoughts is a separate matter from entertaining them and dwelling on them. When they come, dismiss them and replace them with the truth. If, however, you accept what that negative voice is saying, they will derail your dreams. Your goals won't happen. *Period.*

That voice is a part of life, but it should not have the last word. You have the power to silence your doubts by speaking life to your situation. Unless you do this, unless you talk to yourself, your dreams will go nowhere. "Talk to myself? Isn't that a little crazy?" you ask. No, but it is radically effective. The Bible itself teaches that what you say to yourself has an impact on your soul. What impacts your soul impacts your life.

Speaking life to your dreams simply means making affirmations about them. Proverbs 18:21 (NASU) says, "Death and life are in the power of the tongue." God is telling us that words matter and have power. He also reminds us through the Scriptures that "kind words are like honey—sweet to the soul and healthy for the body" (Prov. 16:24, NLT). Words have the power to change things, including your health.

Once again, science confirms this. During the 1990s, Dr. Masaru Emoto was inspired to freeze water and capture microscopic images of the crystals after exposing the water to words, prayers, music, and images. The results were incredible! Water that was subjected to negative speech froze into distorted crystals, while water that was exposed to prayer and other positive speech formed beautiful snowflake-like crystals.[37] Similar experiments with plants have showed that plants exposed to negative talk died much faster than plants surrounded with life-affirming words.[38] Add this to what we learned in chapter 1 about how science confirms the connection between our internal thought processes and our external outcomes, and the impact is clear. What we think, say, and believe physically changes our brain chemistry and neural pathways and helps determine the outcomes we experience. What you speak matters.

What we say to ourselves feeds our belief systems. My second Black Diamond failure was not my only experience with self-limiting beliefs. We saw in the last chapter that my postpartum thought that moms always have some belly fat and don't have time to eat healthy or exercise like they once did also sabotaged my desired outcomes for three years. Any progress I wanted to make in the area of health and fitness after the birth of my second child was limited by what I told myself.

In addition to the daily process goals I set and pursued, I also started acting and speaking like I had already accomplished my bigger goals. These were acts of affirmation. I was speaking life into a situation that had seemed dead for three years. Things didn't change overnight, but they changed!

Affirmations are not a quick fix. They might also seem awkward or silly, because our affirmations are often a far cry from our current reality. But this is where the power of the tongue meets the power of the Holy Spirit to move the mountains we thought were immovable. Remember the work of Dr. Caroline Leaf and others who have shown that our words and actions begin in our thoughts? This means that we can use the power of affirmation to change our thought habits.

Before we do that, I want to make sure you're very clear on what an affirmation is. Affirmations have been described as "a declaration that something is true" or "a form of prayer...that is focused on a positive outcome rather than a negative situation."[39] They help us to speak life into our dreams and invite the Holy Spirit to work on our behalf. They create expectations of success within our minds so that our bodies simply follow.

Jack Canfield is recognized as an expert in affirmation. He offers the following guidelines writing your own affirmations. I've added my thoughts in brackets.

- Start with the words "I am." These are the two most powerful words in the English language. [You can use *we are* for affirmations made in unison.]

- Use the present tense [as though it is already happening].

- State it in the positive. Affirm what you want, not what you don't want. [This means that instead of "I don't have debt," you'll say, "I am debt free."]

- Keep it brief. [One-liners are easy to memorize and repeat often.]

- Make it specific. [Vague affirmations produce vague results.]

- Include an action word ending with *–ing* [such as *living, having, achieving,* or *earning*].

- Include at least one dynamic emotion or feeling word [such as *happy, confident,* or *peaceful*].

- Make affirmations for yourself, not others. [The only person you can change is you.][40]

I have used these tips more than once. When I wanted to lose the baby weight, I took my goal, which said, "I weigh a healthy and fit 130 pounds by May 2016," and turned it into the following affirmation: "I am confidently standing on stage giving a presentation at a fit 130 pounds."

My body followed my affirmation by looking for a way to make it happen. A second affirmation of "I am a fit mom, and I thrive at 125" came to fruition in the form of the NPC Central States Bodybuilding Competition and my entry in the bikini division. I decided what I wanted, got clear and excited about it, and the "how" came to mind.

Another affirmation, this time regarding my family relationships, came to fruition through several healing experiences. The affirmation I was speaking over my life and dreams said, "I am so happy and grateful for the victory in my family." The manifestation of it began in my war room. It continued through the experience of our Come as You Will Be Party. The final piece was my decision to participate in a life coach certification course. All of this, combined with my training for the bodybuilding show, gave Brandon and me the space we needed for our relationship to be healed. Soon after this, my affirmation that said, "I am Black Diamond" came to fruition too.

You can speak life over any area, experience, or desire in your life. The following affirmations show how unique and personal they should be. They will also help you become accustomed to the format above:

I am earning money more easily and more quickly every day.

I am happily loving myself just the way I am.

I am feeling great with everything that I do.

I am happily operating my own business from home.

I am proudly accepting my diploma [or new job, or award, etc.].

The beauty of affirmations is that they turn the desires in your head to expectancy in your heart about things you believe you can achieve. When stating your affirmations, you will feel like a kid on Christmas morning—excited, passionate, filled with anticipation, and almost giddy, because you know the fulfillment of your desire is possible. It is just a matter of seeing how God will do it.

A word of advice: keep both goals and affirmations real. They need to ring true and be aligned with your passion and purpose.

Goals or affirmations that evoke anxiety, frustration, or guilt should be set aside and replaced with those that resonate with you. After all, your affirmations are not meant to weigh you down; they are meant to inspire the actions that bring your desired outcomes to pass.

Once you write them down, read your affirmations three times each day: first thing in the morning, in the afternoon, and around bedtime. If you are in a private setting, read them aloud. If not, read them silently. (You can also create voice memos of your affirmations and listen to them often.) Whether or not you speak your affirmations audibly, close your eyes and imagine yourself being in the situation or experience your affirmation describes. Imagine that it is everything you desire and allow yourself to feel the joy of living that part of your dream.

Creating Affirmations

INNER REFLECTION:

When the seed of doubt creeps in and takes over, the only question left to ask is, Will I dust myself off and try again in earnest? These affirmations will help you answer yes confidently and back it up with positive action.

The exercises below are based on the Dream Life goal you created in chapter 9, so have it handy before you begin.

1. Keeping the affirmation format in mind, write down some action words ending in *–ing* that relate to your Dream Life goal. Choose words that powerfully and succinctly evoke your intent. For example, if your Dream Life goal involves public speaking or other forms of influence, words like *inspiring*, *informing*, and *encouraging* might apply. If your goal involves your marriage, words like *rekindling*, *loving*, and *honoring* might capture your desired outcome.

   Action words:

   _____

   _____

   _____

2. Now do the same with words that express your feelings (e.g., *invigorated, excited, strong*) and emotions (e.g., *happy, grateful, content*). (Don't forget that gratitude is one of the strongest emotions, which makes it a powerful way to begin an affirmation and speak life over your goal.)

Feeling words:

_____

_____

_____

3. In the space provided, write down the Dream Life goal and the process goal(s) you chose to focus on in the previous chapter (remember, this is how you're going to work toward your Dream Life goal), and then create affirmations from each.

My Dream Life goal is:

_____

_____

I am _____

_____

I am _____

_____

I am

_____

_____

Daily practice/process goal:

I am

_____

_____

_____

I am

_____

_____

_____

I am

_____

_____

_____

You have created important affirmations, but your work is not done. Writing them down is only the precursor to verbalizing them on a regular basis. If you skip this step, you will deprive yourself of the results you seek. Develop the affirmation habit. It will set you up for massive breakthrough, massive momentum, and massive success.

Eleven

WHAT THE MIND SEES,
THE BODY FOLLOWS

*Plant the seed of desire in your mind, and it
forms a nucleus with power to attract to itself
everything needed for its fulfillment.*

—ROBERT COLLIER

IF AFFIRMATIONS MOVE your goals from your head to your heart,
then visualization cements them in place. After I turned my goal
of "I will hit Black Diamond" into the affirmation "I *am* Black
Diamond," I took it one step further: I started visualizing it.

Being very sure of what I wanted allowed me to see the picture
clearly. I saw our CEO calling Brandon and me to congratulate us
on going Black Diamond. I pictured us at the company's annual
conference, where the leadership recognized our achievement. As
I envisioned these events, I thought about how a Black Diamond
leader would act, and I began doing the things a Black Diamond
leader would do. For an entire month, I wore a jacket that said
"Black Diamond" for every team webinar.

Involving my team in the vision caused them to rally, which
generated additional energy and momentum and more success for
them. Creating this collaborative space caused all of us to become

more strongly bonded together. I believe that this increased unity invited the Holy Spirit to work among us.

Throughout all of this, I experienced the emotions connected to the success I envisioned. Before long, these positive emotions overshadowed the fear-based ones that had tried to own me. This emotional connection to the goal affected my outlook, helping me to see myself through Black Diamond eyes before I was Black Diamond.

Mind you, thoughts of fear and doubt never vanished completely. (I am human, after all!) However, I worked at consciously choosing my thoughts, focusing on the positive and visualizing the outcomes I wanted to achieve. With the help of my team, I regained control over the positive-negative balance of thoughts in my head and tipped it toward the bright side.

Then it happened! On September 1, 2015, our CEO called to say that we'd achieved Black Diamond! As my eyes filled with tears, I took a deep breath and savored the moment. The call that I had visualized countless times had come, and it went exactly the way I pictured it!

POWER IN A PICTURE

Visualization is powerful because it creates a mental image of what we want. This is in keeping with how our minds work, because we think in pictures. Our thoughts unfold like movies; as we watch them, they impact our physical bodies, emotions, and perceptions of the world.

Children know this instinctively. Do you remember using your imagination to become a superhero who saves the world or a basketball star who makes the winning shot? Did you imagine being a mother, doctor, or firefighter? Did you turn your living room into a Broadway stage and perform for your parents and family? Do you remember experiencing the joy of your imagined success?

For children, imagining such things is invigorating; but somewhere along the line we adults begin using our imaginations to envision worst-case scenarios. The childhood minds that explored exciting outcomes and exotic places now conjure up scenes of fear and dread. Frantically we ask, "What if I can't pay my bills? What if I lose my house? My job? My health? What if I don't get well?" Because the body does not discriminate between real and imagined threats, the terrors gripping our minds can lead to physical manifestations of panic. The scenario might be fictional, but the body's alarms are triggered in very real ways. In other cases, these terrifying scenarios manifest in real life. (Remember, what we think about, we bring about.) This confirms our fears and keeps us stuck in this pattern.

Avoiding such torment is not as simple as denying your bad thoughts. Have you ever tried *not* to think about the gruesome movie scene that seems imprinted on your mind? The harder you try not to think of it, the more you become obsessed with the idea because you are focused on it. The solution to negative thoughts is not thought avoidance but thought replacement, which means choosing to focus on something you want to envision and experience.

For my dream of hitting that Black Diamond promotion, I had to choose whether I would live in my doubts or replace them with mental pictures of victory. Either one would become self-fulfilling prophecies! I knew which way to go, but breaking out of the negative mind-set was not so easy. After two years of bitter disappointment over the promotion I failed to make, my mind was hardwired with the fear that I would be disappointed again. Clearly, I had work to do!

Chances are, you do too. Every time you berate yourself saying, "I try to lose weight, and I never do," or, "Nobody wants what I have to offer," you create a mental picture that supports a negative outcome and opposes your dream. No one can change that mental picture for you. You must decide which self-fulfilling prophecy you want to experience!

Train Your Gatekeeper

What you visualize affects how your brain works, whether for your dreams or against them. Here's how: At the lower part of your brain, a group of cells called the reticular activating system (RAS) serves as an information gatekeeper. Its job is to determine which data is most relevant and important to you. The RAS then brings that information to your attention, to the exclusion of most anything else.

The deselection powers of the RAS are formidable. Of the eleven million bits of data that bombard your senses in any given moment, you might consciously perceive only forty.[41] The whittling down is based on clues you provide. Those clues are your thoughts. If you spend a lot of time worrying about whether you will lose your job, your RAS ranks similar thoughts as being the most relevant to you. When those thoughts appear at the door of your mind, your information gatekeeper ushers them in. As the saying goes, you get what you really want.

Think about the last car you bought. Once you decided on a certain make and model, it seemed to show up every place you went. The car had been there all along, but when your RAS recognized your preference, it unlocked your awareness and caused that car to stand out. Simply put, your subconscious mind knew the car was important to you, so it began looking for the car and for ways to make it yours.

What are you currently visualizing? Is it something you desire or the very thing you dread? Is your mind filtering out positive options because you are focused on the negative ones? If so, you can train the gatekeeper in your brain to heighten your awareness of thoughts that support your dream. You do this by creating strong mental pictures of what you want your life to look like. That will send your subconscious on a quest to make it happen.

Ready? Let the quest begin!

INNER REFLECTION:

The exercises in this section will work with your Dream Life goal and corresponding affirmations, so keep them handy. The visualization you are about to create will help train your brain so that your RAS searches not for your fears but your dreams.

1. Write down your Dream Life goal and affirmations again so that your subconscious mind can beginning focusing on the life you want to live.

My Dream Life goal is:

_____

_____

I am _____

_____

I am _____

_____

I am _____

_____

I am _____

_____

I am _____

_____

I am _____

_____

2. Based on your stated goals and affirmations, visualize what your life will look like. Then describe it in narrative form below. Remember to write in the present tense, as though you have achieved it and are living it today. As always, be detailed and specific and include your senses (sight, touch, smell, sound, and taste), emotions, and feelings.

_____

_____

_____

_____

_____

_____

_____

_____

_____

_____

_____

_____

Picture what you wrote daily. It will help you to replace negative thoughts with the life picture you desire. It will also remind your RAS to highlight thoughts and images that are congruent with your stated dreams.

The next step is to expand your vision by inviting others to join you on this journey, thereby unlocking the power of collective consciousness and teamwork. The Bible says, "For where two or three gather in my name, there am I with them" (Matt. 18:20). Sharing your visualization has real effects, as the quantum theory of entanglement reveals. The law describes a physical phenomenon occurring when groups of particles interact as though they were one. It suggests that "even if you separate entangled particles by billions of miles, changing one particle will induce a change in the other."[42] Likewise, when we share our experiences, we share our emotions and gain a louder voice.

As we open ourselves to the Holy Spirit during these life-giving exchanges, we are empowered by Him to impact the world around us in ways that are disproportionately greater than our numbers and abilities. That means that with the Holy Spirit involved, two plus two equals a lot more than four!

3. With whom have you shared your vision?
How did sharing it affect your progress?

_____

_____

_____

_____

_____

_____

4. Become consciously aware of those who are
on the journey with you. Ask yourself who
is already helping you to propel your vision
forward. Write their names in the spaces
provided and briefly describe the nature of
their support.

	WHO IS WITH ME?	HOW ARE THEY WITH ME?
1		
2		
3		
4		
5		

WHO IS WITH ME?	HOW ARE THEY WITH ME?
6	
7	
8	
9	
10	

5. Support/partnership is not always warm and fuzzy. You need trustworthy confidantes who are willing to get in your business at times. So ask yourself, "Who is by my side, holding me accountable?" Write down his/her/their names and briefly describe your level of openness to them.

_____

_____

_____

_____

_____

_____

6. If no one is holding you accountable, explain why not and write down the names of three people you might involve in this way.

_____

_____

_____

_____

_____

_____

The power of visualization is not solely about dreaming. It is about unlocking the power of your sub-conscious mind so that you can become the person you were created to be. The more consciously aware you become, the more empowered you are to live the way you long to live—to your fullest, most mind-blowing potential.

Twelve

LIVE IT OUT

The secret of success is found in your daily routine.
—JOHN MAXWELL

YOU KNOW ABOUT the mom belly that left me feeling insecure after the birth of my second child. At the start, the steps I took to get my body back to its prepregnancy state seemed inadequate to vanquish the final few pounds. I wrote down my personal fitness goal, created affirmations and visualizations surrounding it, and wrote my goal weight—"130, 130, 130"—on the shower wall each day. For too long, nothing changed.

I worked out and watched what I ate. No brownies. No sneak binges. No excuses. Still, the scale would not budge. After months of focusing on my goal, it was still between five and ten pounds out of reach.

Have you ever wanted something that badly, given it the proper focus and effort, and seen no progress at all? The slightest movement in the right direction would have given you hope and motivated you to keep going. What you wanted was some evidence—*any* evidence—of progress.

I know how it feels. When there's no evidence, it can be hard to stand strong. I nearly caved, wondering whether I should accept my lot and embrace my extra weight as my new normal. I thought about chalking it up as an inevitable outcome, blaming childbirth and a busy mother's lack of free time. To consummate my surrender, I could hit the couch, grab the remote control, and pound down some brownies. After all, *not* eating them had done me no good.

The whole gamut of self-defeating thoughts tempted me. Deep down, however, I knew a belly was not what I wanted. I would *have to* find a way to lose it, and my approach would have to be different from anything I'd tried up to that point. Frustrated as I was, I was in a good place—the place where the status quo is disturbing enough to make difficult changes look attractive.

The popular definition of *insanity* is "doing the same thing and expecting different results." Based on that definition, most of us are insane. Like rodents in hamster wheels, we keep repeating the same failed actions. It's as though, instead of making healthy changes and taking appropriate actions, we'd prefer to complacently wait for miraculous changes to meet us where we are. Then we complain like crazy when those changes don't come.

To experience change, we need to *make changes*. That means taking action that supports our desired goals. It also means recognizing that some actions are more beneficial than others.

ARE YOUR ACTIONS FORCED OR EMPOWERED?

What motivates our actions has an impact on their effectiveness. Therefore, two types of actions—forced actions and empowered ones—have two different outcomes.

Forced action is all about the *shoulds* in our minds and the compulsion to make something happen. Have you experienced the emptiness, exhaustion, demotivation, and limited results that forced action produces? Do you know anyone who has operated in this way, working themselves to the bone, grumbling the whole time but accomplishing little?

How can you produce positive outcomes by doing what you hate, focusing on the problem instead of the solution, being miserable, and wearing yourself out both physically and emotionally? No amount of forced action can create real momentum or abundance, apart from a boatload of nervous energy. Thinking you should do something is not a formula for successful living.

If you are in that space right now, be encouraged. There is a way out! Instead of trying to make something happen, act when you feel inspired to do so. That kind of action is empowering. It addresses issues from an abundance mind-set and a sense of alignment with passion and purpose. It will make you more open to change, no matter how uncomfortable that change might be. Instead of releasing nervous energy, empowered action will foster healthy energy fueled by excitement, joy, and enthusiasm.

Good things seem to happen effortlessly when you act in inspired ways. Time flies, and when your task is finished, you feel pleased with what you have accomplished. Instead of dreading the next step, you rejoice at the prospects. You become the master of your calendar. This creates consistent habits that increase momentum in the direction of your dreams, turning empowered action into inspired results.

Empowered action is what rescued me from treating my goal like a magic wand I could wave over my weight issues so they would melt away. It helped me admit that diet and exercise were not cutting it. I acknowledged that if I wanted a leaner body, I would have to make some changes. That's when I made a drastic change and did something I had *never* done before. I began to seriously train for a bodybuilding competition. This was far enough out of my comfort zone to push my mind and body past their stuck points.

Entering the competition was not something I felt I *should* do to reach my goal. It was an empowered action that led to new opportunities, and it lined up perfectly with my passions. It was exciting, but it was also uncomfortable much of the time. Nevertheless, I was committed to doing whatever was necessary to restore my prepregnancy body. It paid off. My so-called "mom belly" went the way of the dinosaurs, and I got an important lesson on the power of taking the right kind of action.

HABITS MATTER

Have you noticed yet that you are a reflection of your daily habits? Some of your habits are obvious. You probably drink the same coffee each morning, and you might even eat the same breakfast. Your workouts are probably similar each week, and you shop in your favorite stores more often than not.

Without a doubt, I am a creature of habit. Some habits are good, helping me to organize my days in somewhat predictable patterns that eliminate a lot of unnecessary decision-making. Being on semi-autopilot has consequences, however, because unless I examine and reassess my habits, my automatic choices can send me in directions I don't really want to go.

One of my favorite books is Darren Hardy's *The Compound Effect*. Hardy deals with the long-term impact of habits and suggests that a "1-percent" adjustment can lead a person down an *entirely* different path.[43] His book is a reminder that not all change has to be earth-shattering. Small, incremental change is still change, and it adds up significantly.

Consider two women who work and have small children. The first woman is Tracy. Each day, Tracy comes home from work tired and stressed. She wants nothing more than to rest her weary mind, so she grabs some chips and ranch dip from the kitchen and sinks into her most comfy chair to watch thirty minutes of her favorite TV show.

Thirty minutes later, the stresses of work are behind her and she feels relaxed—so relaxed that she stays in her comfy chair and watches another show. At least five days a week, thirty minutes of unwinding becomes sixty, much of it accompanied by snacking. Tracy doesn't realize that her daily habit is taking her somewhere.

She might not recognize the correlation when, ten years later, she is overweight, lethargic, and unmotivated.

Now meet the second woman, Liz. She comes home from work equally tired, stressed, and needing to unwind, except she takes a thirty-minute walk around the neighborhood. Afterward, she feels so relaxed that she decides a longer walk would feel even better. So, five days a week she walks as much as an hour, often while praying or greeting her neighbors.

At some point, Liz goes from walking to jogging and joins a triathlon group. She's athletic and fit, feels healthy and strong, and meets likeminded friends who encourage her in her pursuit of her passions. She is more connected to herself and to God, so her relationships are more connected too. She experiences a higher degree of success because she is full of joy. For Liz, life is good and business is booming.

Habits really do matter! The same thirty- to sixty-minute time frame led each woman down a completely different path. This should encourage us! It means we can change the direction of our lives by changing our habits incrementally. We can begin by addressing our schedules.

Schedule Power

Setting and sticking to a schedule is powerful. To train for the bodybuilding show, I had to rearrange my calendar. My goals had shifted, so I reworked some of my time commitments. This helped me make time for new workouts and meal-prep needs.

Scheduling is an act of intention. To reach my goals, I had to know exactly when I would work out and what I would eat. Without intentionality, I would end up someplace, but not the place I wanted to be. With it, I could create a game plan that would support new habits, which would in turn support my bodybuilding dream.

If you invest time in creating a schedule, your schedule will help ensure that your goals are met. Once my schedule was in place,

I did not question whether I should I go to the gym. I just went. I didn't have to make choices or play mind games with myself. I simply stuck to the plan. Soon I got used to the new schedule and kept it almost without thinking about it. You can get to this point too. Here are some tips to help you:

- If your goal has a deadline—for example, if you want to lose a certain amount of weight by a specific wedding or vacation date—start with that date in mind and work backward, deciding how much weight you intend to lose each month and how you will lose it. Add to your calendar whatever activities are needed to achieve the goal.

- The same idea applies to a business goal (for example, a certain sales or production figure) that must be achieved by a specific date. Start with the end date/result in mind and decide what monthly, weekly, and daily activities will support your goal. Add them to your calendar and keep the commitment going.

- If you find calendar items that are no longer helping you reach your goals, remove them from your calendar. You are free to stop good things so that you can do great things. For example, when Brandon and I were building our business, I had to say no to our volleyball team, youth group, and other hobbies so I could focus on activities that supported our goals.

- Arrange your schedule so that any tasks related to your Dream Life goal are addressed earliest each day. Each night before bedtime, write out the Dream Life goal action items that you will complete, preferably before noon the following day. These are your inspired choices. You are not forced to do them; you get to do them.

You will find that when you do the things that are connected to your life's purpose, you will be full of passion and what I call *end joy*. Even when you don't feel like doing the daily activities your goal demands, doing them will leave you feeling excited and reenergized. This is how you know you are moving in the right direction.

MY SUBTLE SHIFT

If the smallest shift in your habits can transform your total life picture, how can you resist doing it? I can't, so I consistently tweak my habits, create new ones, and eliminate the ones that have outlived their usefulness.

One new habit was to drink a gallon of water a day. I knew people who drank that much water, so I asked them how they did it, how they kept track of their intake, and how it was working for them. Then I figured out what would work for me. I bought a forty-eight-ounce reusable water bottle and planned to drink it down and refill it three times each day, which would elevate my intake to just over a gallon. Now I habitually drink one bottle between 9:00 AM and noon, one between noon and 5:00 p.m., and one after 5:00 p.m. Drinking less than a gallon of water each day would seem weird to me!

Breaking habits is as important as starting new ones. My daily sugar intake with my morning coffee got my attention. I was a Starbucks-o-holic and would sometimes buy three grande-sized drinks at a time to save trips back to the store (although I never shied away from visiting Starbucks). I can remember taking my children out in snowstorms just to get my brew. Whenever we were on vacation, I always made sure I knew where the nearest Starbucks was.

I was an addict with very specific tastes. Regular brewed coffee did nothing for me. What I wanted was a nice, creamy latte loaded with a flavored syrup. When I realized that the syrup was standing between me and my training goal, I realized I was going to have to make a change. So I started asking fitness nuts and black coffee lovers about their coffee-drinking habits. I knew the fitness crowd wasn't loading up on milk and sugar, and I knew the black coffee drinkers managed to enjoy it their way.

That was when I began experimenting with my daily coffee. Instead of my latte, I now add protein powder, a splash of almond milk, and stevia to black coffee. With the exception of an occasional treat, the only barista serving me coffee is me. I make it at home and add my special ingredients. The end result is delicious, and the occasional latte is not a goal-breaker.

My updated water and coffee habits are minor shifts that have taken me in a completely different direction over time. Is there a small change like this that you could make in order to see big results in support of your goal?

Don't Go It Alone

I have learned that when I want to do something that breaks the mold, I cannot do it alone. The idea became a no-brainer when I realized that what I had been doing on my own to lose weight wasn't working and hadn't worked for a long time. So I decided to ask for help. Training for a bodybuilding competition was uncharted territory anyway, so I needed guidance from people in the know. Having that guidance and sharing my intentions with key people in my circle empowered me to do the work that had to be done.

Empowered action is not solo action. Whatever the field of endeavor, there are people in place to help you if you will look for them. If empowered action is aligned with your goals and passions, and it is, then asking the right people for referrals, information, support, money, or time can build a bridge toward your goals faster than anything you could build alone.

The key is to ask, as a college friend of mine learned firsthand. Connie attended one of my webinars in which I teach the skills covered in this workbook, including the power of asking. Below, in her own words, Connie shares the story of how asking transformed her quest:

> About a year ago I was drowning in credit card debt and a mortgage I couldn't afford. I was paralyzed with fear, frustration, and stress and had no idea where to start. After confiding in a friend, the solution seemed so simple: Start with the *ask*. I began making phone calls and asking creditors what my options were and how each party could help me get back on track.
>
> I asked until I got a solution. Then I moved on to the next problem and continued asking until there was a solution. Now I've lowered my mortgage payment by $400 per month and closed two mediocre life insurance plans, which helped me completely pay off one credit card and put some money aside in savings. I replaced my life insurance with a plan offering much better coverage and benefits. In addition, another credit card is now at zero-percent interest and under a payment plan. Another card will be paid off soon.

Connie could not change her banks' credit card rates, but she did what she could. She asked for help. When she did, good things happened. People who had access to information, resources, and referrals offered her solutions that she could not effect alone.

The idea is to start where you are, with what you have. When I decided that other people's input could help me make the changes necessary for reaching my fitness and bodybuilding goals, I asked trainers at my gym if they could help me with meal planning, and I started a challenge group with them to learn about portion sizes and macronutrients.

Then through what seemed like random happenstance (though I no longer believe anything is truly random), I connected with an old friend who was in the final week of training before her bodybuilding show. She had lost more than sixty pounds and looked amazing. She obviously had a handle on the lifestyle skills that I needed to learn. I picked her brain clean, asking her tons of questions about what she had been learning, who she learned from, and what she recommended. I also asked about any pitfalls she had run into during her yearlong adventure. Within a week I was scheduled for my first show and had signed up with a coach that she recommended.

This is not rocket science. When I said I wanted to make a fitness change and lose those last five to ten pounds, I had no idea what the how-to would look like. I most certainly did not envision a bodybuilding show. I simply shared that I wanted to lose weight. When I started asking for help, the bodybuilding competition appeared on my radar screen and changed my trajectory.

Inviting others to help me increased my opportunities to take empowered action and thrust my journey into high gear. Asking for referrals and ideas saved me tons of time, effort, and energy and made the quest infinitely more enjoyable.

Think about one of your current personal goals. Do you know someone who has access to information you need? Has someone been in your shoes and achieved the goal you are working to reach? Why try to reinvent the wheel when they have developed tools and resources that will save you hours of time? Help is available. Just ask.

INNER REFLECTION:

Not all habits are created equal. The first step in choosing the right habits is to distinguish them from the ones that do not actively serve your intent.

1. Which habits are working against you, and how? (These might include your time management, sleep schedule, approach to eating, work habits, fitness routines, relational issues, etc.)

_____

_____

_____

_____

2. What small change can you make right now? Write about how such a tweak could change your life over time.

_____

_____

_____

_____

To own your schedule you have to be brutally honest about what is working for you and what is keeping you confined to your comfort zone. (Remember the examples of Tracy and Liz.) Your current state reflects your use of time. Look at your current schedule and scrutinize your time expenditures. (If you don't have a written calendar, download the free template at DeniseWalsh. com/action.)

3. Which of your time commitments are non-negotiable (e.g., work schedule and family commitments)?

_____

_____

_____

4. Which commitments are out of balance, with too much or too little time dedicated? Do any new items need to be added to your schedule? Subtracted?

_____

_____

_____

_____

_____

_____

5. Which time commitments support the Dream Life goal you established in chapter 9? How much time is dedicated to this goal each week? Is the commitment sufficient? What schedule changes need to be made to better serve this goal?

_____

_____

_____

_____

_____

_____

   Now it is your turn to take empowered action. Think about your current Dream Life goal and the logistics of achieving it. Do you need funds to help launch a business? A babysitter who can free up some time for you to pursue a hobby or go on a date with your spouse? Do you need mentoring or advice about materials? Or would having someone clean your house free you up to make some real money? As you answer the questions below, remember that what you need is usually on the other side of your ask!

6. Think about the people you know. Who might have information, resources, or referrals that can help launch you in the direction of your goals? Don't prejudge their availability or willingness to help. Just jot down

their names and contact info in the spaces provided.

NAME	CONTACT INFO

7. Do you know people who have achieved the goal you are currently pursuing, or a similar goal? Write down their names and the question(s) you would ask each of them.

NAME	THE ASK

8. Add your asks to your schedule. By what date do you plan to contact the people who might be able to help you? Put that date in your calendar or planner and take action!

PHASE #4

Turn Roadblocks Into Stepping Stones

Thirteen

FREE YOURSELF FROM FEAR

God has not given us a spirit of fear, but of
power and of love and of a sound mind.

—2 TIMOTHY 1:7, NKJV

HAVE YOU EVER watched someone do something so incredible that it inspired you to dream bigger? Was your inspiration shattered within seconds by the dream-stealing thought that said, "But I could never do that"?

It takes awareness and determination to neutralize dream-stealers. That's part of why I so admire people who live their dreams. Whether they are Olympic athletes or singers who can belt it out on stage, they have contended with the same intimidating thoughts as everyone else—and overcome them. I don't see their fears. All I see is their passion, and it reminds me that my dreams are possible too.

What dream can you remember carrying in your heart? Are you living it? If not, how and when did you set it aside? My guess is that your dream was cut short the way all dreams are: by limiting beliefs that control your thoughts and keep you from moving forward. But don't despair; your limiting beliefs are not unusual. Everyone has them, and they usually sound something like this:

"I could never do that."

"I'm not that kind of person."

"I'm too _____ to do that."

"I'm not _____ enough to do that."

If you cannot identify with these thoughts or fill in the blanks in the last two, you are probably unaware of the limitations you are placing on yourself. The truth is, you have self-limiting thoughts, and they will hold you back from being your best self, even if you are not consciously aware of them.

Can I get really personal about this? I am consciously aware of my self-limiting thoughts. If I listened to all of them, I would not be living my entrepreneurial dream. I would be on my couch stuffing down brownies and binge-watching home renovation shows on HGTV. My dream life could not have happened on autopilot. I had to consciously design it, partly by identifying and letting go of whatever was holding me back.

One major obstacle was the fear that flared whenever I imagined a better life for myself. For example, while I was in college, I dreamed of impacting disadvantaged teenagers. My idea was to start a high-ropes course that would empower teens to improve themselves and others. There was no doubt that my idea was valid. I knew it could be effective. Yet every time I thought about ways to make it real, fearful thoughts paralyzed me. For a year I took no action. Then another year went by. Graduation day came and went. Soon, school was over, I got my first job, and my dream slipped even further out of reach.

Listening to my fears kept me from doing what I wanted to do. This led to feelings of guilt and resentment. I felt guilty because I wasn't living like the amazing person I imagined I could be. I soon resented myself and anyone who managed to overcome their fears and act on their dreams.

Does this scenario sound familiar? Do you feel the guilt and resentment I felt? Do you see how my journey of entrepreneurship, the one that allowed me to realize my dreams, would never have happened unless I freed myself from my fear?

Getting free meant radically rewiring my brain so that I could stop reacting to my fearful thoughts in self-defeating ways. Notice that I did not say I would stop having fearful thoughts. Instead, I would stop being ruled by them. I admit that it's easier said than done. But it can be done!

Before I decided in favor of entrepreneurship, the thought of failing at a business endeavor filled me with fear. I had to dig deeper to find the fear that was underlying the one that surfaced. I realized that I was not just afraid of failing; I was afraid of what people would think of me if I failed. So I turned the tables on fear and started replacing negative thoughts with excitement at the possibility of becoming more successful. As I did this, I became more convinced that entrepreneurship was what God planned for me.

Then, just when I thought I had it all figured out, more negative thoughts popped up. This time, I wasn't afraid of failing but of succeeding. To be successful would mean having to grow as a person. I wondered how other people would react to my growth. What if they disapproved? And how in the world would I explain a leap into entrepreneurship after getting a master's in clinical psychology?

Perhaps scariest of all was the idea that growth would change my thoughts and perceptions, which would change me as a person. I feared that personal growth might hurt my relationships. What if friends and loved ones didn't like the new me?

The barrage of self-limiting thoughts seemed endless. Soon I realized that I feared being seen. The idea that others would watch my journey and follow me as an example only made me more uncertain of my worth. If people saw me, they might judge me. Would they think I deserved to be followed? As they say, the higher up the flagpole you go, the more exposed you are. The idea of being more engaged with people led to worries that their good opinions of me would wear thin over time.

Obviously, I was way too worried about what other people thought. I have since learned that my only responsibility is to focus on what I am called to do. That means staying in alignment with my dreams and desires and acting accordingly. Whatever people might think, feel, or experience is not on me but on them. As long as I am aligned with God's purpose, all will be well.

After years of practice, being afraid of what other people think seems silly to me. That doesn't mean I never have those old, fearful thoughts. Now, however, I see them from a broader perspective. I've learned that true friends will stick with me regardless of my successes and failures. Those who turn away when the chips are down probably weren't my friends in the first place.

Maybe you can relate to feeling unworthy and not good enough. Maybe you're battling a consuming fear of failure, success, rejection, being laughed at or ridiculed. What are your go-to fears that stop you from being seen and stepping into your gifts? These things will stop your dreams before you even get started, and none of them are real. Trust me; I know from experience. But now that we know better, we can do better, and we can actually assess if these are true or helping us on our path.

Retake Control

Any thought that tells you that you are not good enough is fear based and a lie. The way to take back control is to realize that such thoughts are almost always invalid.

For example, when you feel like you haven't measured up, remind yourself that failure is in the eye of the beholder. If you are doing your best, learning and growing through your efforts, can anyone really say that you have failed? If you are moving toward the goals you set, are you not experiencing success? (This is why goal-setting is so important. It gives you clear guideposts to measure your progress and refute invalid ideas about failure.)

There is another aspect of the fear of failure that needs to be mentioned. It involves the dread of being rejected. In my network marketing business, I realized a long time ago that the idea of being rejected by prospective customers is essentially a myth. If someone opts out of becoming my client, I've lost nothing. He or she wasn't my customer in the first place, so nothing has changed. I move on and keep talking to other people about my business. Those who become customers will have more impact on my success than those who don't, but there is no downside in sharing what I have to offer. Until I learned this lesson, fearing negative outcomes only wasted precious time that could have been used to get my business started and growing sooner.

My strong advice is not to let fear postpone your dream, even a little bit. Fear is a thief and a liar, as the following acronym reveals:

- False

- Evidence

- Appearing

- Real

That is so accurate! The truth is that we make ourselves afraid. We react to our fearful thoughts by seeing them as evidence of impending failure. Then we use them and other "evidence" to confirm and validate what we are thinking. We need to shift this approach radically. Yes, we need to be *aware* of our fearful thoughts, but we need to question our fears' so-called evidence.

Doing this means observing our thoughts before we react to them. Observation shows us that our thoughts are just that: thoughts. They aren't based in reality but in our thinking. They tend to focus on worst-case scenarios, even though such scenarios are among the least likely of all outcomes.

Scrutinizing our fearful thoughts is especially important because our bodies cannot distinguish between real situations and imagined ones. That means scary thoughts affect our bodies virtually the same way scary situations do.

Can you see the importance of carefully weighing your thoughts before you act on them? Until you examine their quality and validity, your responses and actions cannot be accurate, which will prevent you from reaching your goals and stepping into your dreams. Fearful thoughts work against forward motion and encourage the emotional paralysis that avoids stress at all cost. Positive thoughts do the opposite; they encourage you to take actions that will ensure a more beneficial outcome. *In fact, the taking of action is how you overcome your fears.*

There is no silver bullet for dealing with fearful thoughts. You deal with them one thought and one day at a time. That is one of the big lessons I learned in my first ten years as an entrepreneur, and it's one of the reasons I was able to earn multiple millions. I have also learned the following truths:

- My fears are a normal part of living a full life. The only way to avoid them is to stagnate.

- My fears are not true. They occur in my imagination, and I don't have to take them seriously.

These ideas have helped me to separate myself from my fears and anxieties and focus on more productive pursuits: the emotions I want to feel, the life I want to lead, and the person I want to become. Fear never goes away completely, but once I look it in the eye, it loses its power to rule me. Instead, I rule it. You can learn to do the same!

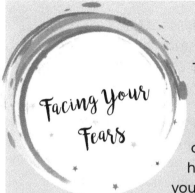

INNER REFLECTION:

The exercises throughout this book are helping you become more consciously aware of the thoughts that are bouncing around in your head and of how they are hurting or helping you. It's time to evaluate your fear-based thoughts so that when you sense them creeping into your mind, you can replace them with thoughts that are aligned with your goals.

1. Complete the sentences below by describing the things that keep you up at night:

I am afraid that

_____.

I am afraid that

_____.

I am afraid that

_____.

I am afraid that

_____.

I am afraid that

_____.

I am *most* afraid that

_____.

Bravo! Identifying these fears is a huge step forward. Your next step is to understand them better and to realize that they are subject to change. The following questions will help you gain power over your fears.

2. Why are you afraid of the situations you listed in question 1? What underlying fears (e.g., of success, failure, rejection, being judged, changing yourself, leaving others behind, etc.) make these scenarios frightening to you?

_____

_____

_____

_____

_____

3. How would overcoming these fears change your life?

_____

_____

_____

_____

_____

4. What practical steps can you take to conquer these fears?

_____

_____

_____

_____

5. Have you ever held yourself back from pursuing an idea, goal, or dream? What specific thought(s) held you back?

_____

_____

_____

6. We learned earlier about taking our thoughts captive in order to transform our minds. Let's do that right now. Write down the fears you listed in response to the first question in this section. Then write down a self-affirming thought with which to replace it. (See the examples, below.)

FEAR-BASED THOUGHTS	SELF-AFFIRMING THOUGHTS
I'm not good enough. Who will listen to me anyway?	I am doing what I have been called to do.

FEAR-BASED THOUGHTS	SELF-AFFIRMING THOUGHTS
Do I even know what I'm talking about?	Every day and every way, I am getting better and better.
Who do I think I am?	I am doing what I love.
Who will listen to me anyway?	I am happy and grateful for this experience.

_____

_____

_____

_____

_____

Reflect on your self-affirming thoughts throughout the day. Write them on sticky notes and place them on mirrors, the fridge, and other places where you will see them often. Write them in your journal too. The more consistent you are at speaking and meditating on these affirmations, the more likely they are to replace your fears and become your beliefs.

Fourteen

GET PAST GUILT AND RESENTMENT

With everything that has happened to you, you can either feel sorry for yourself or treat what has happened as a gift. Everything is either an opportunity to grow or an obstacle to keep you from growing. You get to choose.

—WAYNE W. DYER

IMAGINE THIS: YOU'RE flying over the ocean in a helicopter surrounded by some of your favorite people. The wind is blowing on your face as you watch the sun disappear and reappear behind white, fluffy clouds. Then on the horizon you see your destination: the lush private island where you will spend the weekend in luxury as the guest of honor. For the last few months, you've worked more than sixty hours per week, stretching yourself and the limits of your soul to focus on your goal, and it paid off. You earned a promotion that took you to the pinnacle of the large company where you work, and the CEO personally invited you to his island to acknowledge your success and accomplishment. How do you feel in that moment? Are you filled with pride? Overjoyed at your accomplishment? Bursting with gratitude?

I lived that scenario, and I have to confess: instead of glowing with pride and joy, I was racked with guilt and anxiety. The celebration itself and everything about it was incredible. It was called the

Black Diamond Event, and it included a $5,000 shopping spree, a helicopter ride to my CEO's private island, and other crazy experiences that were more fun than I ever imagined. And believe me, in the years I spent working toward that promotion, I had spent a lot of time visualizing what it would be like to celebrate such a hard-earned accomplishment. The reality truly exceeded everything I had hoped for. Yet there I was, finally the top earner in the company, and I found myself utterly distracted from the celebrations by shame.

While everyone around me partied, I fixated on why Brandon and I had earned the title when others worked harder or needed the victory more. I thought, "I really don't deserve this, and everyone knows it. They're probably mad at Brandon and me for experiencing such success, and I'm pretty sure they want us to fail." I tried to smile proudly, but inside I was battling an onslaught of negative, soul-sucking thoughts.

Thankfully, that weekend wasn't the first time I had experienced this kind of self-sabotage. And thank God my clear-headed husband was beside me to speak truth in the face of the lies. When I shared my guilty feelings with him, he said, "That doesn't make sense, because you know these people as your friends. Everyone in the company is happy for you, even if they were working toward that promotion. You deserve this because you worked hard, and you're teaching others how to succeed." Brandon helped me redirect my invalid fears and focus on the truths that I had temporarily lost sight of.

When the fears returned several hours later, his example and a little outside help got me over the hump again. I knew I had to reject the anxiety and guilt I knew were false, yet I struggled to do it. Just when I wasn't sure how much longer I could resist, I received a text message from one of my team members. She wrote, "Even if I never make another dollar with my business, my life has been changed. My family is closer to God, and I am growing in confidence. I will be forever grateful!"

That text arrived when I needed it most and rescued me from the undertow of negative, self-sabotaging thoughts. The woman who sent it was a third-shift worker at her job who awakened from sleep to express her appreciation. I believe that God woke her up and inspired her to message me just when I needed it most. Her words helped me to break free from my doubts and cemented the idea that people's thoughts about me were not the negative ones I imagined.

In that moment, I realized that I was doing exactly what I was put on planet Earth to do. Therefore, I was free to accept whatever blessings my work produced. It was so freeing!

THE GUILT TRIGGER

My negative reactions to a very positive promotion happened when something inside me was triggered, producing a response that was mismatched to the situation. It had nothing to do with other people. It was all about thoughts and beliefs that predisposed me to feel guilty.

Guilt is a powerful emotional trigger that results from your beliefs about how you should or should not be or behave. Most guilt is misguided, but not all of it is negative. A healthy sense of guilt can move you in a new, more positive direction. But unchecked guilt can keep you stuck in the past and unable to move forward.

The important thing is to be aware of any guilt and to offer yourself forgiveness for any wrongdoing that is causing it. That is the best way to be healed. Remember, you cannot change your past, but you can change your *view* of the past. Forgiveness is the key to doing so.

The Bible doesn't address forgiving yourself, but it does say that God forgives you. First John 1:7 says, "If we walk in the light, as he is in the light, we have fellowship with one another, and the blood of Jesus, his Son, purifies us from all sin." Jeremiah 31:34 states "'No longer will they teach their neighbor, or say to one another, "Know the LORD," because they will all know me, from the least of them to the greatest,' declares the LORD. 'For I will forgive their wickedness and will remember their sins no more.'" If guilt has been pervasive in your life, it is time to accept the Holy Spirit's gift of freedom and forgive yourself!

THE RESENTMENT TRIGGER

Resentment builds when you feel others have wronged you in some way. Unless the issue is dealt with in a healthy manner, resentment festers and forms an underlying anger that never seems to quit. Even if you have been hurt—grievously hurt—resentment is no way to live.

Here again, the healing agent is forgiveness. The Bible challenges us to forgive others over and over again. When Peter asks Jesus, "'Lord, how many times shall I forgive my brother or sister who sins against me? Up to seven times?' Jesus answered, 'I tell you, not seven times, but seventy-seven times'" (Matt. 18:21–22).

Forgiveness is not about condoning or accepting other people's wrong behavior. Nor does it mean that your feelings aren't justified. Forgiveness is about healing yourself and releasing the negative emotions that would otherwise keep you from the life you were born to live.

Depending on the situation, you might choose to forgive but opt out of remaining in relationship with the person who hurt you. That doesn't mean you can circumvent forgiveness. Without forgiveness, painful emotional ties could continue, even after the relationship is severed. You don't want to carry emotional baggage that will hinder your growth and success in the future. Guilt and resentment, like jealousy and bitterness, are like poisons you drink expecting the other person to die.[44] In reality, they will hurt *you*.

JEALOUSY AND COMPARISON

Earlier in the book I confessed to the comparison game I got caught up in for a bit after Brandon and I started our business. Well, comparison has a cousin named *jealousy*. If you let them, these two will keep you more focused on other people's lives than on your own, making it impossible for you to step into your own dream.

Comparison usually revolves around other people's accomplishments and wondering deep inside whether you are good enough to be like them and do what they do. To remedy this, you try to become them by internalizing their behaviors. The problem is that you were not created to emulate anyone; you were created to follow your own passions.

Jealousy is about looking at the outside of someone else's life and wanting what you see. Have you been there? I have! With the help of someone who cared enough to tell me the truth, a recent case of jealousy ended in a dream fulfilled. But it started with the green-eyed monster eating my lunch.

It happened when a friend of mine launched a podcast. The same idea had been on my mind for years, so when my friend got it done, I was jealous. A friend called me out on it and said, "Well, I guess she's making it a priority and you're not." Ouch! She was right. I hadn't made time for a podcast. Really, the idea intimidated me, which is probably why I kept it on the back burner for so long. When my friend got there first, I turned green. I'm happy to say that identifying and dealing with my jealousy led me to start my podcast, *Dream Cast*. Instead of allowing myself to become paralyzed with envy, I looked inward, examined my own goals and motivations, and got to work.

Really, jealousy is a signal that someone else is prioritizing a dream that is important to you but is languishing in your life. If you are upset because someone else is getting fit or has a great relationship or is working toward an important goal, use your jealousy to your advantage. Plan how you will get more of what you want. Make room for it in your life. Prioritize it, get it on your calendar, and kick the green-eyed monster to the curb!

EMOTIONAL BAGGAGE

Fear, jealousy, and the comparison trap will hold us back, but so can past experiences. They can taint our vision of ourselves and our world and become the emotional baggage that impacts whatever we do. Unless we deal with these experiences in healthy ways, layers of negativity can hinder our forward motion.

Emotional baggage is triggered when someone or something touches an already sensitive area. I want you to consider a somewhat oversimplified, fictional example of how this works. Imagine that you check your hair in the mirror one morning and leave home satisfied that it looks OK. You meet a friend for coffee, and she makes a puzzling comment about your blue hair color. Would the remark upset you? Or would you laugh and think your friend was just being silly?

Your response would depend upon what you thought about your hair before your coffee date. In this case, you would probably tell your friend, "I'm not sure why you're saying that. My hair isn't blue!"

Now imagine the story with an added twist: When you left your colorist the day before, you thought you detected the slightest hint of blue in the mirror, but you brushed off the idea thinking it was your imagination. Today, your friend's remark confirms your suspicions, and you exclaim, "Oh no! I thought I saw blue tones. My colorist messed up. I can't believe I paid money for this! I'm going to demand a redo." Because your conversation over coffee connects with your earlier concerns about your hair, you are tempted to go down an emotional rabbit hole of embarrassment, resentment, and anger. Your prior experience positioned you for a strong emotional response.

Here's a personal example: Some people in my life probably think I travel too much. Part of my work involves going on two- or three-day trips to train my team or speak at events. I typically do this a couple of times a month. If deep down I agreed that I travel too much, or if I secretly worried that my travel was keeping me from being the sort of mother I want to be, people's comments about how frequently I am away from home might send me into an emotional tailspin. But because I see the issue differently, I don't overreact to outside opinions on this matter. Sure, I have felt guilty at times about missing one of my kids' games or after-school activities. But I choose not to live in a place of guilt. I have wondered, "Do I travel too much? Am I a bad mom?" But I choose not to allow those worrisome thoughts to consume me. The reality of our family's schedule tells another story. Because of the freedom my work provides, I get to pick up my boys from school every day, and we have tons of fun time together each afternoon. I can provide things we could never afford if I didn't travel as part of my work. When I realize this larger truth, I'm not triggered by remarks about my travels.

You don't have to be burdened by emotional baggage. To be free of it, however, you will need to identify your areas of sensitivity and work through them. Figure out why you are so reactive and then put the issue in perspective. When triggers are neutralized, you can act on your positive goals, move past negative emotions, and eliminate the reactions that work against your purpose.

A final thought: emotional triggers breed in the things you tell yourself. You are not triggered by what others say and do but by how you already feel about yourself and your situation. This is another good reason to train the voice in your head to speak positively. If your thoughts are habitually negative, you will be overly sensitive to people's words, and you will experience unnecessary turmoil.

Let's throw all our emotional baggage overboard! The rewards will be enormous.

INNER REFLECTION:

Receiving Healing and Walking in Freedom

Getting free is about being healed, whether physically or emotionally. Getting healed emotionally happens when you look within and challenge the voices and experiences that are holding you back. So let's unmask some general triggers that may be at work in your life.

1. What do you feel guilty about? What expectation did you violate or fail to live up to?

_____

_____

_____

_____

_____

_____

_____

Remember that emotional responses (anger, anxiety, frustration, jealousy, etc.) signal areas in need of healing. Just as you named your fears in the previous chapter, it's now time to identify

your feelings of guilt. Keep in mind that guilt is rooted in your beliefs about how you should or should not be or behave. Begin to uncover hidden areas of guilt by answering the following questions.

2. What is unrealistic about that expectation?

_____

_____

_____

_____

3. What is the underlying assumption or belief that is at the core of that expectation?

_____

_____

_____

_____

_____

_____

_____

4. Can you change your past behavior?

_____

5. How can you get rid of this guilt? (If you find yourself truly stuck, see the endnote for my suggestions.[45])

_____

_____

_____

_____

_____

_____

_____

6. Healing reframe: Consider one issue that has caused a healthy sense of guilt, and check which statements accurately apply to your past, present, or future behavior.

— I did my best with the information I had at the time.

— Now that I know better, I will do better.

— I am not the same person I was then. I am committed to continued growth and better future outcomes.

We can use healthy guilt to learn and grow, but we certainly don't want to stay stuck there. Using the guilt as a tool to learn, grow, and pivot is called conviction and helps us to better ourselves and our lives.

7. How do the statements you checked empower you to overcome guilt?

_____

_____

_____

_____

Now let's pinpoint any areas of resentment by answering the following questions.

8. What expectation of yours did someone violate or fail to live up to?

_____

_____

_____

_____

_____

_____

_____

9. What is unrealistic about that expectation?

_____

_____

_____

_____

10. What is the underlying assumption or belief that is at the core of that expectation?

_____

_____

_____

_____

_____

_____

_____

11. Can you change their past behaviors?

_____

12. So how can you get rid of this resentment? (Once again, if you find yourself stuck, see the endnote for my suggestions.[46])

_____

_____

_____

_____

_____

13. Can you change the people you resent? Can you change their behavior or choices? Why or why not?

_____

_____

_____

14. Healing reframe: Check the statements that (1) accurately apply to those you have resented and (2) allow a more complete view of their actions.

— They did their best with the information they had at the time.

— They didn't know what they didn't know.

— I might have done the same in their situation.

You might not get to the bottom of these issues in one sitting, so revisit these pages from time to time. This is part of the work of emotional freedom. Your answers provide clues to the inner work you need to do. The more willing you are to go there, the more you will learn about yourself and the patterns that are constraining you. The more you know, the more you can change yourself and your life.

There are costs for not accomplishing the inner work that brings freedom. But when negative thought habits are broken, you will gain the emotional space and energy your dream life demands!

Fifteen

CHANGE YOUR ENVIRONMENT

*The secret of change is to focus all of your energy,
not on fighting the old, but on building the new.*

—DAN MILLMAN

So FAR THE pitfalls we have discussed are found within you—
feelings of fear, jealousy, comparison, guilt, and resentment.
Now it's time to turn your focus outward toward your environment. Why? Because changing your environment changes you,
for better or for worse.

We know that our decisions have an enormous effect on our
outcomes, but some of what we think, feel, and do is a response
to our environment. Often, this is an area where we don't control
our thoughts and actions as well as we might, because we don't
recognize the effect that outside factors are having on us. When
your environment thrives, it positively impacts your physical body,
inner life, and every function of your being. When it doesn't, it can
swallow your vision, passion, and activity toward your goals whole.

So what do I mean by *environment*? For our purposes, it is about
the context within which we experience life. In that sense, environment includes the following:

- *Our interactions with others.* Family, friends, and the
  communities with which we interact provide us with

a rich tapestry of experiences that impact and influence us.

- *Our surrounding physical environment.* Our homes, workplaces, and other spaces in which we spend time affect us, whether we realize it or not.

- *Our physical body/health.* The health of the body (including our fitness, nutrition, and energy levels) affects our choices, interactions, and activities.

Let's see how these aspects of environment function and how we can maximize them to achieve the great outcomes we desire.

INTERACTION WITH OTHERS

As the saying goes, no man or woman is an island. Everything you have learned through this book will ultimately affect and be affected by your interactions with others. Even your habits, good and bad, are affected by others. Journalist and author Charles Duhigg says, "For a habit to stay changed, people must believe change is possible. And most often, that belief only emerges with the help of a group."[47] That is the power of community, "even if that community is only as large as two people."[48]

The power is real because we connect to others through emotionally charged experiences and shared adventures: siblings grow up together, college buddies take road trips, coworkers gossip at lunchtime. (I didn't say all of the connecting was positive.) These shared experiences produce shared emotions, which cause us to bond with one another, not just emotionally but also neurochemically.

Once we bond emotionally with another human being, our subconscious works to match us to that person by changing our physicality and outlook. You probably know people who are very close and who share similar energy levels, mannerisms, and perspectives. As long as these qualities remain matched, the bond holds, because each party is receptive to the other's emotional state.

Sometimes the bonding process is accelerated by dramatic or even traumatic events. Have you ever wondered how couples on reality romance programs "fall in love" within days of meeting one another? It is not because they have finally found their one true love but because they have shared an emotionally charged, exhilarating experience. Such events create strong emotional bonds in short periods of time.

Most bonding experiences occur over longer time frames, which allows for more fluctuation in the relationship. Let's take the fictitious example of a woman named Sam and her coworkers, who meet in the lunchroom almost every day. As they eat, they groan about never-ending paperwork, husbands who won't help with the housework, and a certain team member whose work ethic is not up to snuff.

Sam and her lunchroom friends have become emotionally bonded, not around feel-good experiences but around negative emotions and a sense of victimization. They relate easily to one another because all of them are stewing in the same emotional juice. As long as they stay under its power, they will stick together and look forward to their lunchroom gripe sessions.

One day, after some self-reflection, Sam has an epiphany. She realizes that the lunchroom scene is bleeding negativity into the rest of her day and that the communal whining is no longer serving her purposes. She understands that it is not harmless but is enforcing a sense of victimization.

Sam wants out. So she heads toward the lunchroom with a different mind-set. When her friend Ellie launches into a rant about the coworker who never makes a dent in the workload, Sam tries to change the subject, saying, "Let's not talk about her today. What fun things have you planned for this weekend?"

Ellie is dumbstruck. "What is wrong with you today?" she asks Sam. "Are you mad at me?"

Sam's reaction startles Ellie because it doesn't match the negative energy they usually share—the emotional bond that connected them in the first place. Instantly, Ellie becomes insecure about their friendship. "Are you still my friend?" she asks. What Ellie is really asking is, "Are we still compatible as friends?"

Sam has a choice to make, and it will help to form her future. She has three options. She can:

bow to the negativity in order to maintain the status quo in her relationships;

stay on her new positive path and try to make the lunchroom scene more uplifting; or

she can avoid the lunchroom habit altogether by eating at her desk, going for a walk, or choosing new, more optimistic friends who match her changed emotional state.

Our relational environments are teeming with seemingly insignificant conversations that drastically impact our emotions, focus, and drive. Friendships deeply impact our views of the world, our workplace, our family, and ourselves. Entrepreneur, author, and speaker Jim Rohn has famously suggested that in terms of personality, temperament, and worldview, we become the average of the five people we associate with most. Only we can decide which emotional ties are serving our purposes and which need to be set aside.

We sometimes fail to make the tough decisions about negative (and even toxic and dangerous) relationships because emotional bonds are the most difficult to break. Often, we feel obligated to those who are no longer good for us but have been there to support us in the past. This is especially true of those with whom we have been close for a long time.

In the end, we are 100 percent responsible for choosing relationships that serve us well. Some relationships are so toxic that continuing at all would be hazardous. In less extreme cases, we can establish emotional boundaries so we don't internalize the other party's unhelpful moods and emotions. It is even possible, over time, that others will embrace the optimism we model and slough off their negative ways. But that is entirely their choice.

When I felt stuck at my mental health job, I was part of a small group at church. Choosing to connect with positive, like-minded, goal-focused, and God-filled people kept me in the land of dreams instead of drama. Had it not been for these dreamers and doers, I would not have had the faith or courage to step out into a new career. Because I bonded with positive thinkers who breathed life into my thinking, I moved in the direction of my dreams.

This landed me in a whole new community of people, and I showed up every chance I got. How it changed me! I learned to dream because I was hanging around with dreamers. I learned to finish what I started because I was hanging out with people who accomplished what they set out to do. Because I was in a place where I could grow and receive feedback, I also learned to stop doubting my ability to add value and inspire others. I created new habits and beliefs because I was involved in a community that believed in developing them. You could say their belief rubbed off on me.

For better or worse, others' beliefs rub off on you, too, affecting not only your attitude and focus but your mental and physical health. It's not surprising then, that isolation (the lack of community) puts you at an even greater risk factor for disease[49] than stress, which is said to prompt "up to 90 percent of all visits to primary care physicians."[50]

There is no way around it: relationships matter. If you are in the wrong community or are isolated from community, make a decision. You are not a tree stuck in a patch of ground. If your current relational environment is not working for you, change it! You get to decide which people will impact and influence you. In other words, you become like the friends you pal around with, so find people you want to be like and go hang out with them.

The Physical Environment

Did you ever try writing with a dried-out pen, only to toss it back into the drawer angrily? How did you feel when you picked it up the next day and repeated the whole frustrating process?

That pen represents your physical environment and its effect on you. If your environment is in good shape, life gets easier. But if you are surrounded by broken tools and other annoyances, your environment is causing you unnecessary stress and distracting you from your goals and dreams. It could eventually overwhelm you.

Here's the good news: if you will quit tolerating them, you will find that most of your environmental problems are easy to fix. For example, do you have a messy garage, office, or car? Are unfinished projects staring you in the face? These issues don't have to consume the brain space that would be better used elsewhere. Just make a decision to bring them into order!

When Brandon and I first realized that we were squandering mental energy over little inconveniences, we became less tolerant of them. One day Brandon said, "We have two children, and it drives me nuts every morning to use the toaster twice for their toast!" He was right. Our mornings are busy, and a simple four-slice toaster could make them easier. So Brandon ordered one online. It was such an easy fix, but it saved my husband valuable emotional energy each and every morning—and it got me thinking about the little things that bugged me every day.

One of my pet peeves was how all the stuff on my passenger seat—my laptop, food, water bottle, and purse—flopped onto the car floor when I hit the brakes. How many times had my food spilled and my water bottle rolled out of reach? Finally, I made a change. I arranged my items on the floor of my car, but within reach. Problem solved. Frustration over!

What daily annoyances are you tolerating? Is it a nagging technology issue or something that never moves off your to-do list? It might seem inconsequential, but these squatters are occupying real estate in your brain. Kick them out by optimizing your physical environment. Organizing your life, even a little bit, can create an easy flow and turn your environment into a comforting and serene space. Clean out your files and shred the piles of documents you no longer need. Replace wire hangers with solid wooden ones and watch what happens. Beautify your space with flowers, pictures, candles, or whatever is pleasing to your eye. Add the right music, and your heart will soar!

Improving your environment requires intention. You have to decide to create a space you love. When it's done, you will have made room in your head for more important things, like achieving your dreams.

PHYSICAL BODY AND HEALTH

Take any cell from your body, put it in a petri dish filled with toxins, and guess what? That cell will die. Put the same cell in an oxygen- and nutrient-dense environment, and it with thrive. It's up to you to create an environment in which every cell in your body can flourish.[51]

What you eat determines what kind of energy your cells are getting, which impacts your hormones, inflammation, gut and digestion issues, and more. You are what you eat—literally. Science is confirming that good food is real medicine for preventing illness. Eating a balanced diet of fresh food, including fruits and vegetables, gives your cells what they need for good health.

I know this can be a tender subject for many people, and I realize that combing through the nutritional information can be daunting. But I've learned that you can simplify matters simply by tracking your daily intake. What you can track, you can change, and it's easy to do with some basic journaling. Just write down the foods you typically eat throughout the day and ask yourself, "What can I work on in this area? What changes would benefit my health?" Then act on the dietary tweaks you need to make. You can use this information as fuel for creating a specific Dream Life goal and process goals to support it. (Refer back to chapter 9 for the steps to turning your desire into specific, actionable goals.)

Hydration is another key issue that is often overlooked. Now that my hydration habits are good, I notice the change when I forget to take my water bottle with me. Drinking plenty of water is critical for keeping cells healthy. It's not surprising then that I'm mentally quicker and clearer when I am staying hydrated. I cannot emphasize it enough: stay hydrated!

Another factor affecting your physical condition is rest. Sleep allows your body to heal and repair your heart, blood vessels, and muscles. Ongoing sleep deprivation can lead to an increase in health concerns, including high blood pressure, kidney disease, and diabetes. It can also increase anxiety, darken your mood, cause weight gain, and increase the signs of aging. To get your rest, you have to plan for it. Find a bedtime routine that works for you and stick with it.

Obviously, each of these topics deserves a book of its own. The point here is to be aware that how you manage your environment impacts your life overall, including your mood, focus, and drive. So, go ahead! Use the exercises below to assess where you are and make these changes so that you can begin to reap surprising rewards.

INNER REFLECTION:

Your relationships

Community is vital, yet we are often passive about our relationships. In the questions below, let's take an inventory of the community with which you are connected. Note that this is less about social media friends than it is about those friends with whom you have ongoing and personal interaction.

1. Who do you call when you have a problem or need advice?

_____

2. Do you call that person by force of habit or because the relationship is fruitful? Explain.

_____

_____

_____

_____

3. Who are the five people with whom you spend the most time?

1 _____

2 _____

3 _____

4 _____

5 _____

4. In response to each of the following questions, place a plus sign (+) or minus sign (−)
   next to each name you listed above.

   — Does time spent with this person inspire you or
     discourage you?

   — Does this person make you want to be a better
     person? A happier person? A more successful
     person?

   — Does this person help you to achieve your most
     important goals?

   — Does time spent with this person boost your joy or
     drain you of energy?

The plus and minus signs should speak for themselves. Consider which relationships are in your best
interests and which are not and make adjustments
accordingly.

Your surroundings

Next, shift your focus to your physical environment.

5. Tour your house, car, and office and ask
   yourself, "What irritates me about this
   space? What causes unnecessary stress?
   What lingers on my to-do list but never
   gets done?" Write down your answers in
   the space provided.

_____

_____

_____

With the above responses in mind, ask yourself the following questions and answer them in the space provided:

6. What can I do to eliminate the irritation, relieve the stress, or complete the task?

_____

_____

_____

7. Who can I ask for help?

_____

_____

_____

8. What has kept me from accomplishing this task sooner?

_____

_____

_____

9. What benefit will result from accomplishing it now?

_____

_____

_____

10. By what date will I ask for any needed assistance, and by what date(s) will I finish the task?

_____

_____

_____

Your health and wellness

The easiest way to improve your eating habits, water intake, and sleep quality is to start a journal. To make it even easier, use one of the many diet and fitness tracking apps available, as well as fitness tracking watch or other device.

11. What diet changes have you made? (Be specific about foods you have eliminated, substituted, replaced, or reduced.) How have these changes established better eating habits?

_____

_____

_____

_____

_____

_____

12. What is your typical sleep schedule? What changes will you implement to improve the quality of your sleep and ensure that you are not sleep deprived?

_____

_____

_____

_____

Once you have turned these behaviors into habits, you can keep building onto them. Remember, subtle, incremental change is still change, and it compounds to result in big changes, especially when you target the one area of your life that most impacts the others.

Conclusion

KEEP DREAMING

WAY TO GO! You have made great strides since starting this workbook. You assumed control of your thought life and shifted your mind-set to be conducive to the life you want to lead. You clarified your desires and stated your intentions. You have become a person who makes goals and commitments and follows through. You finish what you start. You know how to make hard choices and course corrections to keep your eyes on the destination and your feet on the path toward your purpose. With these accomplishments, you have already changed your life and your family's legacy—and all simply by changing yourself.

Do you sense the shift that is already taking place in your life? Can you tell how much closer you are to living the life of your dreams? I hope so!

I also know sometimes it can be hard to perceive your own progress. That's why I asked you to take a questionnaire in the introduction that would serve as a baseline against which you can measure just how far you've come. It is your "before" picture. Now let's take a snapshot of where you are today. Complete the questionnaire once again, and notice the addition of a couple of new questions.

Celebrating Forward Progress

INNER REFLECTION:

1. Describe your life situation, including your health, relationships, career, and overall satisfaction, as of today.

_____

_____

_____

_____

_____

_____

_____

_____

_____

_____

_____

_____

_____

_____

2. On a scale of one to ten (with ten being the most positive rating), what are your levels of joy, peace, and happiness in each of the following seven categories?

Family   1 2 3 4 5 6 7 8 9 10

Friendships   1 2 3 4 5 6 7 8 9 10

Finances   1 2 3 4 5 6 7 8 9 10

Health   1 2 3 4 5 6 7 8 9 10

Hobbies   1 2 3 4 5 6 7 8 9 10

Business   1 2 3 4 5 6 7 8 9 10

Giving back   1 2 3 4 5 6 7 8 9 10

3. Write the names of the three important people you listed in the introduction. On a scale of one to ten, rate the quality of each relationship.

Name _____ 1 2 3 4 5 6 7 8 9 10

Name _____ 1 2 3 4 5 6 7 8 9 10

Name _____ 1 2 3 4 5 6 7 8 9 10

4. Which of your initial hopes have you fulfilled through completing this book?

_____

_____

_____

_____

_____

_____

_____

_____

5. What desired changes have you seen in yourself and your life situation as a result of completing this book?

_____

_____

_____

_____

_____

_____

_____

6. Describe several aha moments you experienced throughout these pages.

_____

_____

_____

_____

_____

_____

_____

7. How have these revelations affected your perspectives, actions, and outcomes?

_____

_____

_____

_____

_____

_____

_____

8. Who can you share your epiphanies with? Teaching what you have learned is another way to solidify its effects.

_____

_____

_____

_____

_____

_____

_____

_____

9. Please attest to your answers with your signature and today's date below.

Sign _____

Date _____

Perhaps you noticed that while I referred to your responses in the introduction as a "before" measure, I didn't call these answers your "after." That's because while this chapter marks the end of the book, it is still just the beginning of your story.

If you weren't already, you are now a dreamer, and because of what you've learned and applied through your journey so far, you are growing closer and closer each day to the person you were created to be. By allowing your passions to bubble up into your conscious awareness, you have made them your focus, so that your purpose is clear and your action is inspired. It is paying off. With each breakthrough you achieve and every perceived ceiling you shatter, you will evolve into a more powerful and more fulfilled human being.

Don't stop here.

This book is not about undertaking a one-time overhaul but about changing yourself and your life one step at a time. This incremental process is less daunting—who wants the pressure of having to achieve perfection in one, perfect shot?—and more inspiring, and if you continue, the compound effect of your gradual tweaks will utterly transform your life.

So revisit chapter 9 every quarter. Choose another area of life to work on, and begin the process again. Each time you do, new vistas will open up, and new adventures will begin. Bad days will become a thing of the past, and your dream life will grow closer and closer. Every time you give yourself the space to practice the exercises in this book, you will evolve into a more nuanced, connected, and compassionate version of yourself.

It takes hard work to dig this deep on a daily basis, but when you do, you grow more fully into the person you were created to be, and you live closer to your highest purpose. I have seen one dream after another become reality for those who take the steps to get there. It has happened for Brandon and me, for people close to us, and for people whom we have yet to meet.

I firmly believe that it is in your power to be among their ranks.

You can experience your dream life if you will commit to it. You can thrive in all areas at once and be an encouragement to others. More importantly, you are worthy of blossoming into the person God created you to be. In fact, I believe it is your duty to do so.

So, my fellow dreamer, don't stop dreaming, now or ever. Each time you dream purposefully and take action, you become more attuned to yourself and to God. Continue to grow, always evolving into the person you really are: one who positively impacts the world just by being fully yourself.

Dream on, my friend. Dream on!

Notes

One: Thoughts Matter—a Lot!

1.   Though the exact authorship of this quote is often disputed, the earliest printed attribution points to Frank Outlaw, now-deceased president of the Bi-Lo supermarket chain. For more information, please consult https://quoteinvestigator.com/2013/01/10/watch-your-thoughts/.

2.   All statistics in this paragraph are quoted from "Show #412: Success Programming for Your Brain," Ziglar, August 24, 2016, https://www.ziglar.com/show/successprogrammingforbrain/.

3.   "Appendix D: Artificial Neural Network," web.mit.edu, accessed November 2, 2017, citing the work of Donald Hebb presented in his book *The Organization of Behavior: A Neuropsychological Theory* (New York: Wiley, 1949).

4.   David Mielach, "We Can't Solve Problems by Using the Same Kind of Thinking We Used When We Created Them," *Business News Daily*, April 19, 2012, http://www.businessinsider.com/we-cant-solve-problems-by-using-the-same-kind-of-thinking-we-used-when-we-created-them-2012-4.

5.   *Blue Letter Bible* Hebrew Lexicon Online, s.v. "Strong's H8085-*shamaʿ*," accessed March 27, 2019, https://www.blueletterbible.org/lang/lexicon/lexicon.cfm?strongs=H8085&t=kjv.

6.   Caroline M. Leaf, Brenda Louw, and Isabel Uys, "The Development of a Model for Geodesic Learning: The Geodesic Information Processing Model," *The South African Journal of Communication Disorders* 44 (January 1, 1997): 53–70. For more information on Leaf's impressive work, see "Dr. Leaf's Research," Dr. Leaf, accessed April 9, 2019, https://drleaf.com/about/dr-leafs-research/.

7.   Merriam-Webster Online, s.v. "geodesic," accessed November 2, 2017, https://www.merriam-webster.com/dictionary/geodesic.

8.   According to Daniel G. Amen, "Noticing the good is much more effective in changing behavior than noticing the bad." *Change Your Brain, Change Your Life: The Breakthrough Program for Conquering Anxiety, Depression, Obsessiveness, Lack of Focus, Anger, and Memory Problems* (New York: Harmony Books, 2015), 126.

TWO: REPROGRAM YOUR BRAIN FOR SUCCESS

9.   http://michaelbalchan.com/braininfrastructure/?hvid=4s4TeL

10.   Michael Balchan, "Use Brain Anatomy to Your Advantage."

11.   Jack Canfield, "Take 100% Responsibility for Your Life," in *The Success Principles: How to Get from Where You Are to Where You Want to Be* (New York: HarperCollins, 2005), 3–22.

12.   Canfield, *The Success Principles.*

13.   Caroline Leaf, "The Science of Thought," in *Switch on Your Brain: The Key to Peak Happiness, Thinking, and Health* (Grand Rapids, MI: Baker Books, 2013).

14.   "Serenity Prayer," The Prayer Foundation, accessed December 20, 2017, http://www.prayerfoundation.org/dailyoffice/serenity_prayer_full_version.htm.

THREE: AWAKENED WITH GRATITUDE

15.   Oprah Winfrey @oprahwinfrey, "Be thankful for what you have and you'll end up having more.," Facebook, October 3, 2011, https://www.facebook.com/oprahwinfrey/posts/10150372378472220.

16.   Matthew P. A. Fisher, "Quantum Cognition: The Possibility of Processing With Nuclear Spins in the Brain," *Annals of Physics* 362 (November 2015): 593–602, https://doi.org/10.1016/j.aop.2015.08.020.

17.   Jack Canfield, "Six Daily Habits of Gratitude That Will Attract More Abundance and Joy into Your Life," *Jack Canfield Maximizing Your Potential* (blog), accessed October 25, 2017, http://jackcanfield.com/blog/6-daily-gratitude-habits-that-will-attract-more-abundance-and-joy-into-your-life/.

18. Canfield, "Six Daily Habits of Gratitude That Will Attract More Abundance and Joy into Your Life."

19. Canfield, "Six Daily Habits of Gratitude That Will Attract More Abundance and Joy into Your Life," *xvi*.

20. Leaf, *Switch on Your Brain*, 194–195.

21. Randy A. Sansone and Lori A. Sansone, "Gratitude and Well Being: The Benefits of Appreciation," *Psychiatry (Edgmont)* 7, no. 11 (November 2010): 18–22, https://www.ncbi.nlm.nih.gov/pmc/articles/ PMC3010965/, and "In Praise of Gratitude," Harvard Mental Health Letter, November 2011, https://www.health.harvard.edu/newsletter_ article/in-praise-of-gratitude.

22. Taylor W. Schmitz, Eve De Rosa, and Adam K. Anderson, "Opposing Influences of Affective State Valence on Visual Cortical Encoding," *Journal of Neuroscience* 29, no. 22 (June 03, 2009): 7199–7207, https://doi.org/10.1523/jneurosci.5387-08.2009.

23. "31 Individual Healings of Jesus Christ," Strong in Faith, accessed October 25, 2017, http://stronginfaith.org/article. php?page=111.

FOUR: ALIGNMENT LEADS TO ACHIEVEMENT

24. Larry Dossey, *Prayer Is Good Medicine* (San Francisco: HarperOne, 1997), cited in Caroline Leaf, *Switch on Your Brain: The Key to Peak Happiness, Thinking, and Health* (Grand Rapids, MI: Baker Books, 2013), 114.

25. Andrew Newberg and Mark Robert Waldman. *How God Changes Your Brain: Breakthrough Findings from a Leading Neuroscientist* (New York: Ballantine Books, 2010), 26–27.

26. Joe Dispenza, "Meditation, Demystifying the Mystical, and Waves of Your Future," in *Breaking the Habit of Being Yourself: How to Lose Your Mind and Create a New One* (Carlsbad, CA: Hay House, 2013). Dispenza's explanations of brain function are helpful to our discussion. As far as meditation is concerned, biblical meditation is the practice I endorse.

27.   Omar Singleton et al., "Change in Brainstem Gray Matter Concentration Following a Mindfulness-Based Intervention Is Correlated With Improvement in Psychological Well-Being," *Frontiers in Human Neuroscience* 8, no. 33 (February 18, 2014), https://doi.org/10.3389/fnhum.2014.00033.

28.   Richard Davidson and Antoine Lutz, "Buddha's Brain: Neuroplasticity and Meditation," *IEEE Signal Processing Magazine* 25, no. 1 (January 1, 2008): 176–74, https://doi.org/10.1109/msp.2008.4431873.

29.   *War Room*, directed by Alex Kendrick (Culver City, CA: Sony Pictures Home Entertainment, 2015), DVD.

FIVE: YOUR JOY POINTS TO YOUR PASSIONS

30.   "Motivational Quotes," Success, accessed December 19, 2017, https://www.success.com/article/19-quotes-about-following-your-passion.

31.   Shawn Achor, *The Happiness Advantage: The Seven Principles That Fuel Success and Performance at Work* (London: Virgin, 2011), 78.

32.   Achor, *The Happiness Advantage*.

33.   Achor, *The Happiness Advantage*.

SIX: YOUR PASSIONS POINT TO YOUR PURPOSE

34.   Jim Rohn, "Jim Rohn's Goal Setting Challenge," SUCCESS Academy, accessed April 10, 2019, https://jimrohn.successacademy.com/goal-challenge.

NINE: TURN YOUR DREAMS INTO PLANS

35.   Edwin A. Locke et al., "Goal-Setting and Task Performance: 1969–1980," *Psychological Bulletin* 90, no. 1 (1981), 125–152, https://pdfs.semanticscholar.org/8008/47819f1663e1d7eff388c8e89168955074b4.pdf.

36. "SMART Goals," Mind Tools, accessed March 31, 2019, https://www.mindtools.com/pages/article/smart-goals.htm.

TEN: THE POWER OF BELIEVING YOUR OWN WORDS

37. Masaru Emoto, *The Hidden Messages in Water* (Hillsboro, OR: Beyond Words, 2004), DVD-ROM; Emoto, "Healing With Water," *The Journal of Alternative and Complementary Medicine* 10, no. 1 (June 2004): 19–21, https://doi.org/10.1089/107555304322848913; Emoto, "What Is the Photograph of Frozen Water Crystals?", The Power of Love and Gratitude Made Visible, accessed October 26, 2017, http://www.masaru-emoto.net/english/water-crystal.html; Emoto, "What Is the Photograph of Frozen Water Crystals?", The Power of Love and Gratitude Made Visible, accessed October 26, 2017, http://www.masaru-emoto.net/english/water-crystal.html.

38. Michael Pollan, "The Intelligent Plant," *The New Yorker,* December 23 and 30, 2013, 92–105.

39. Christine Brooks Martin, *Talk to God With Affirmations of Faith* (self-pub, CreateSpace, 2011), 7.

40. Jack Canfield, "Daily Affirmations for Positive Thinking," *Jack Canfield: Maximizing Your Potential* (blog), accessed December 29, 2017, http://jackcanfield.com/blog/practice-daily-affirmations/.

ELEVEN: WHAT THE MIND SEES, THE BODY FOLLOWS

41. Tor Norretranders, *The User Illusion: Cutting Consciousness Down to Size* (New York: Penguin Books, 1999), 126.

42. Andrew Zimmerman Jones, "Quantum Entanglement in Physics: What It Means When Two Particles Are Entangled," Thought Co., updated July 10, 2017, https://www.thoughtco.com/what-is-quantum-entanglement-2699355.

TWELVE: LIVE IT OUT

43. Darren Hardy, *The Compound Effect: Jumpstart Your Income, Your Life, Your Success* (New York: Vanguard Press, 2010), 60–61.

Fourteen: Get Past Guilt and Resentment

44.   The exact origin of this phrase is in dispute, but the most-quoted version of it—"Being resentful, they say, is like taking poison and waiting for the other person to die"—is attributed to Susan Cheever, in her book *A Woman's Life: The Story of An Ordinary American and Her Extraordinary Generation* (New York: William Morrow & Co., 1994).

45.   You can only truly get rid of guilt by forgiving yourself and, if possible, asking for forgiveness. The former, forgiving yourself, is an interior work that can often be handled alone with determined effort, but if you find you're having a hard time letting go of condemnation and shame, please seek the advice and help of a trained counselor. With respect to the latter, asking for forgiveness, you can do so out loud or in writing. Both are cathartic and valuable.

46.   I recommend writing a letter to the person who hurt you telling them that you have forgiven them. Once you've written it, read it out loud to yourself. After that, you're free to throw the letter out, burn it, or deliver it; it's your choice. However, if you choose to address this person, be mindful that confronting the individual who hurt you can be challenging and painful. In some cases, including those where trauma was the result, it is not advisable. While I am always an advocate for seeking the guidance of a trusted pastor or counselor, their expertise is especially helpful when the goal is uprooting bitterness and resentment. These professionals will also be able to provide wise counsel and direction about whether it is best to avoid or pursue contact with the person who hurt you.

Fifteen: Change Your Environment

47.   Charles Duhigg, *The Power of Habit: Why We Do What We Do in Life and Business* (New York: Random House, 2014), 92.

48.   Duhigg, *The Power of Habit*, 93.

49.   Bruce H. Lipton, *The Biology of Belief: Unleashing the Power of Consciousness, Matter and Miracles* (Hay House, Inc., 2015), 148.

50. Mohd Razali Salleh, "Life Event, Stress and Illness," *The Malaysian Journal of Medical Sciences* 15, no. 4 (October 2008): 9–18, https://www.ncbi.nlm.nih.gov/pmc/articles/PMC3341916/.

51. Lipton, *The Biology of Belief,* 48.